D1985219

Speak Thai Today

Speak Thai Today

a Thai Foundation Course

Ian Fereday
Rattanaporn Pimsuwan

for complete beginners

sentence building

step-by-step

easy to understand

get speaking fast!

สร้างประโยค

พื้นฐานความรู้
คำศัพท์สำคัญ
พูดง่าย เข้าใจเร็ว

Patong Language School

✦ teaching Thai since 1983 ✦

Speak Thai Today

by Ian Fereday & Rattanaporn Pimsuwan
www.learning-thai.com

ISBN 978-616-590-478-0

First edition 2021
Second edition 2022

Printed in Thailand by S Offset Graphics Design

Published by Ian Fereday & Rattanaporn Pimsuwan

© 2022 Ian Fereday & Rattanaporn Pimsuwan

No part of this publication may be reproduced, stored in a retrieval system, stored in a database and/or published in any form or by any means, electronic, mechanical, photocopying, recording or otherwise, without the prior written permission of the publisher.

ห้ามผู้ใดทำซ้ำส่วนหนึ่งส่วนใดของสิ่งพิมพ์นี้ ห้ามเก็บไว้ในระบบหรือฐานข้อมูลที่สามารถดึงข้อมูลมาใช้ และ/หรือเผยแพร่ในรูปแบบใด ๆ หรือด้วยวิธีการใด ๆ ทางอิเล็กทรอนิกส์ เครื่องกล ถ่ายเอกสาร บันทึกหรืออื่น ๆ โดยไม่ได้รับอนุญาตเป็นลายลักษณ์อักษรล่วงหน้าจากผู้จัดพิมพ์

Dedicated to the memory of Mrs Prapasri Fereday; the best Thai language teacher anyone could have had. You taught us so much; this book would not exist but for you and your patient instruction.

Table of Contents

Section 1

Chapter 1

Welcome, information icons, online materials .... Page 2

PLS phonetic Thai alphabet .... Page 3

Consonants .... Page 3

Vowels .... Page 4

Tone rules .... Page 5

Chapter 2

Units & decimals .... Page 7

11 to 20 .... Page 8

Tens & units .... Page 8

100 to infinity .... Page 9

House numbers, postcodes and phone numbers .... Page 10

Simple math .... Page 11

Days of the week .... Page 12

Polite particles .... Page 12

Chapter 3

Personal pronouns .... Page 13

Verbs 1 .... Page 14

Your first sentences .... Page 15

Verbs 2 .... Page 16

Want to & would like to .... Page 17

Here & there .... Page 18

Travelling verbs .... Page 19

Negatives .... Page 21

Conjunction 'with' .... Page 22

Conjunction 'and' .... Page 24

Future tense .... Page 24
Asking questions .... Page 26
Answering questions .... Page 27
Short question form .... Page 28
Chapter 4
Can .... Page 29
Cannot .... Page 30
Can questions .... Page 31
Answering .... Page 32
Exceptions .... Page 32
Chapter 5
Greetings & small talk .... Page 35
Chapter 6
New vocabulary - nouns .... Page 37
Furniture .... Page 37
Food & drink .... Page 37
Clothing .... Page 37
Technology .... Page 38
Miscellaneous .... Page 38
New vocabulary - adjectives .... Page 38
Colours .... Page 40
Using adjectives .... Page 40
Adjectives as verbs .... Page 41
Chapter 7
This & that .... Page 43
Verb-to-be 1 (*bpen*) .... Page 43
Possessive adjectives .... Page 43
Possessive pronouns .... Page 44
Who .... Page 45

Whose .... Page 46
Chapter 8
Verb-to-be 2 (*yùu*) .... Page 47
New vocabulary .... Page 47
Places .... Page 47
Verbs .... Page 48
Where? .... Page 49
Chapter 9
Verb-to-be 3 (*kheuu*) .... Page 51
Negative forms .... Page 51
kheuu .... Page 51
bpen .... Page 52
yùu .... Page 52
Adjectives .... Page 53
Exceptions for colours .... Page 53
Question tags .... Page 53
Chapter 10
Classifiers .... Page 56
New vocabulary - classifiers .... Page 56
New vocabulary - nouns .... Page 57
Using classifiers .... Page 58
Chapter 11
Have .... Page 60
Not have .... Page 61
Do you have? .... Page 62
There is & There are .... Page 62
Want to have/to get .... Page 63
Chapter 12
Quantifiers .... Page 65

Many .... Page 66
Not many .... Page 67
Solitary .... Page 68
Measures .... Page 69
How many? .... Page 71
Chapter 13
Time indicators .... Page 73
Points in time .... Page 73
Modifiers .... Page 74
Parts of the day .... Page 75
Mealtimes .... Page 76
Chapter 14
Question words 'when, 'what', 'why' and 'how' .... Page 78
Chapter 15
Conjunction 'that' .... Page 80
Conjunction 'but' .... Page 83
Chapter 16
Telling the time .... Page 85
Section 2
Chapter 17
Which .... Page 92
'That' as a relative pronoun .... Page 93
Chapter 18
Past tense .... Page 95
Chapter 19
Comparing .... Page 102
Chapter 20
More quantifiers .... Page 110

Chapter 21

Must, necessary, should .... Page 112

Chapter 22

Prepositions of place .... Page 116

Prepositions of time .... Page 119

Chapter 23

Every, except, besides .... Page 123

Chapter 24

If, then .... Page 127

Chapter 25

Give, cause, allow, for .... Page 129

Chapter 26

Also, together .... Page 133

Chapter 27

Making nouns .... Page 138

Chapter 28

Ever & frequency .... Page 144

Chapter 29

Maybe & because .... Page 151

Chapter 30

Prefixes and suffixes .... Page 153

Chapter 31

In the past .... Page 158

Chapter 32

Family relations .... Page 161

Appendix I

Most common classifiers .... Page 164

Appendix II

Most common verbs .... Page 168

Appendix III

Most common nouns .... Page 173

Appendix IV

Most common adjectives .... Page 180

Appendix V

Jobs & professions .... Page 182

Appendix VI

Places .... Page 184

Appendix VII

Months of the year .... Page 186

Thai index .... Page 187

English index .... Page 196

Section 1

In section 1 we'll cover the basic building blocks that make up Thai sentences. You'll learn how to make your own statements and how to ask and answer questions. We'll cover 'can' and 'cannot' and learn how to talk about the future.

You'll learn how to use adjectives to describe objects, and how to say or ask who 'owns' something. With classifiers you'll learn how to count objects in Thai and talk about 'having' something. We'll cover quantifiers to talk about 'amounts' of things and how to measure them.

As well as learning how to tell the time, you'll learn about time indicators and different parts of the day, so you can say 'when' something takes place.

Finally, you'll learn the 'wh-' question words and some conjunctions to complete section 1.

Chapter 1

Welcome!

Thanks for choosing to begin your Thai language adventure with us!

Speak Thai Today is designed for self-study alongside the free online materials or for students working with a Thai teacher. Either way works fine.

There are a couple of things you need to know before getting started.

Information icons

There are free videos, audio files, exercises and quizzes available online. Just follow the link below to log in.

indicates there's an exercise or quiz online

indicates there's video or audio online

Online materials

Simply scan the QR code or visit the website: www.learning-thai.com

SCAN ME

Just select **Speak Thai Today** to get started right away. Click on any lesson in 'curriculum' to be taken to the materials. No signup or enrolment is required, and you'll have lifetime access.

The unit names are listed on the left menu in the order we'll be studying them in the book. You can get started right away with counting, days of the week, pronouns and verbs 1.

If you can't wait to start speaking, jump ahead to chapter 3, but note that you'll need to know your numbers before you get to 'using classifiers' in chapter 10, and know the days of the week before 'time indicators' in chapter 13.

Phonetic Thai alphabet

The following tables are the standardised spellings used in all Thai study books and materials published by Patong Language School. PLS uses a phonetic system that's easy to read whilst still retaining good pronunciation and tone. You can familiarise yourself with the system by listening to the online audio or reading aloud from the book to a Thai friend.

initial consonants

Thai initial consonants are the sounds that begin a syllable or word. They never change their sound, unlike English, where a 'g' may sometimes sound like a 'j'. We can break down the initial consonant sounds to the following alphabet of 20 letters.

g	as in s**k**y	ng	as in ri**ng**	w	as in **w**ant
j	as in **j**ar	n	as in **n**ame	kh	as in **k**iss
d	as in **d**og	m	as in **m**an	ch	as in **ch**at
dt	as in s**t**op	y	as in **y**es	ph	as in **p**et
b	as in **b**og	r	as in bu**rr**o	th	as in **t**in
bp	as in s**p**ot	l	as in **l**ove	f	as in **f**og
s	as in **s**end	h	as in **h**ave		

note: 'ph' & 'th' are soft 'p' and 't' sounds (**not** as in 'phone' or 'thin')

'bp' and 'dt' are hard 'p' and 't' sounds

In fact, the 'bp' combination is neither a 'b' nor a 'p'; it is somewhere in between. The same applies to 'dt'; it is between a 'd' and a 't'. Model yourself on the online audio to master these sounds.

Although 'ng' is often found within or at the end of many English words, having 'ng' as an initial sound is quite difficult for speakers of European languages. Again, practise with the online audio until you get it right.

Thais can sometimes be lazy speakers, dropping some words and shortening others. They often drop the letter 'l', change the 'r' to an 'l' or even drop the 'r'. Some Thais in the central region even change 'kw' to 'f'! We suggest you speak with all the correct letters until you are more confident and in a situation where speaking colloquially will help you fit in.

ending consonants

Not all of the initial consonants are used as ending consonants to end a syllable or word. For example, there are no Thai words ending in 's' or 'ch'. In fact, there are only eight ending sounds; the following six consonant sounds plus 'w' and 'y' attached to vowels that you'll see in the table of vowels below.

m	as in di**m**	n	as in bi**n**	ng	as in ri**ng**
p	as in to**p**	k	as in jo**ck**	d	as in co**d**

vowels

There are two versions of most Thai vowels; a long and a short. Long vowels are drawn out and extended, while short ones are clipped or cut off. Some vowels don't have a convenient equivalent in English, so we've tried to explain how to pronounce them. A smile helps!

long vowels & combinations		**short vowels**	
aa	c**ar**t, heart	a	b**a**t, f**a**d
aai	wh**y**, sk**y**	ai	b**ye**, fl**y**
aao	ch**ow**, p**ow**der	ao	p**ou**t
aeh/ae	p**ay**, p**a**le	eh/e	p**e**t, b**e**nt
aae	**ai**r	ae	c**a**t
aeo	baby w**aeh w**aeh	-	-
er	**lear**n, t**ur**n	uh	d**ir**t
aey	sof**a y**awn	iu	f**ew**
aew	r**ailw**ay	ew	f**ew**
ee	b**ee**t	i	b**i**t, k**i**d
iia	Mama M**ia**	ia	Mama M**ia**
iaao	m**eow**	-	-
oo	g**o**, **low**	oe	p**o**ke
ooi	g**o y**et	-	-

aw	**law**, **tau**t	o	**lo**t
oy	**lawy**er	-	-
uu	b**oo**t	u	p**u**t, t**oo**k
uua	tr**ue a**nt	ua	tr**ue a**nt
uuai	tr**ue why**	-	-
euu	b**oo**t (while smiling)	eu	y**eu**ch!
euua	t**oo a** day (smiling)	eua	t**oo a** day (smiling)
euuai	t**oo why** (smiling)	euai	t**oo why** (smiling)

Tones

Being a tonal language, Thai can be a real challenge when getting started. If the tone is wrong, you risk being misunderstood, but don't get hung up on being tone-perfect though. As long as you're speaking in complete sentences, you'll be understood more through context than pronunciation. Good tone comes with practice and from listening to other people speaking.

tone marks

In our deliberately simple phonetic system we place an accent above the first vowel in a word or syllable to indicate tone. Tones apply to syllables, not words, so a multi-syllable word may have more than one tone mark. Here are the accents you'll see throughout this book:

common tone   lòw tòne   fâlling tône   hígh tóne   rǐsing tǒne

The common tone is spoken at your normal speech level, just as in regular conversation. Words without an accent are common tone.

Lòw tòne words have an accent pointing down to indicate 'low'. This tone is spoken at a level below your normal speech level.

Fâlling tône words have a hat-like accent rising, then falling. This tone is spoken with an inflection; listen closely and you'll notice that Thai speakers increase their tone slightly before falling away. Falling doesn't mean falling directly from common tone, dropping down; it starts from a higher tone *or* is a slight increase from common tone before falling.

Hígh tóne words have an accent pointing up to indicate 'high'. This tone is spoken at a level well above your normal speech.

Rǐsing tǒne words have a U-shaped accent to indicate that the tone drops before increasing, in the opposite way to falling tone. This tone is similar to the rising inflection at the end of a question in English.

Examples in this book

The examples throughout this book are presented in English, with phonetics below and finally Thai script underneath, like this:

English	example
phonetic	dtuua-yàang
ไทย	ตัวอย่าง

Get familiar with the PLS phonetic alphabet by watching the short video online.

phonetic Thai alphabet

Chapter 2

Units & decimals

the numbers 1 to 10

Numbers and counting are an essential part of learning a language. We use them for prices, telephone numbers, house addresses, post codes, calculations, and so on.

Although Thai script has its own unique characters for writing Thai numbers, most of the time you'll only come across Arabic numerals. You won't see Thai numbers very often other than in government documents or occasionally used as a house number.

Take your time learning the numbers as you progress through the rest of the book. You'll need to be able to count up to twenty by the time you get to chapter 10 though!

the numbers 1 to 10

0 -	sŭun ศูนย์	(decimal point) . -	jùd จุด
1 -	nèung หนึ่ง	6 -	hòk หก
2 -	săwng สอง	7 -	jèd เจ็ด
3 -	săam สาม	8 -	bpàaed แปด
4 -	sèe สี่	9 -	gâo เก้า
5 -	hâa ห้า	10 -	sìp สิบ

Numbers after the decimal point are spoken individually, like this:

0.45 -	sŭun jùd sèe hâa ศูนย์จุดสี่ห้า	9.56 -	gâo jùd hâa hòk เก้าจุดห้าหก
5.68 -	hâa jùd hòk bpàaed ห้าจุดหกแปด	3.25 -	săam jùd săwng hâa สามจุดสองห้า

1.6 - nèung jùd hòk
หนึ่งจุดหก

4.92 - sèe jùd gâo sǎwng
สี่จุดเก้าสอง

11 to 20

the numbers 11 to 20

The Thai numbers from 11 to 20 are made by adding the word for 'ten' **in front of** one to nine.

For numbers higher than 10, if 1 is the unit, it is read as -*èd* instead of *nèung*, as you can see in 11 below.

11 - sìp-èd
สิบเอ็ด

12 - sìp-sǎwng
สิบสอง

13 - sìp-sǎam
สิบสาม

14 - sìp-sèe
สิบสี่

15 - sìp-hâa
สิบห้า

16 - sìp-hòk
สิบหก

17 - sìp-jèd
สิบเจ็ด

18 - sìp-bpàaed
สิบแปด

19 - sìp-gâo
สิบเก้า

20 - yêe-sìp
ยี่สิบ

Tens & units

the tens 20 to 90

With the exception of 20 - which is a unique word - units of ten are formed by adding the word 'ten' **after** a unit.

20 - yêe-sìp
ยี่สิบ

30 - sǎam-sìp
สามสิบ

40 - sèe-sìp
สี่สิบ

50 - hâa-sìp
ห้าสิบ

60 - hòk-sìp
หกสิบ

70 - jèd-sìp
เจ็ดสิบ

80 - bpàaed-sìp
แปดสิบ

90 - gâo-sìp
เก้าสิบ

We can then add units like this:

21 - yêe-sìp-èd
ยี่สิบเอ็ด

36 - săam-sìp-hòk
สามสิบหก

52 - hâa-sìp-săwng
ห้าสิบสอง

75 - jèd-sìp-hâa
เจ็ดสิบห้า

41 - sèe-sìp-èd
สี่สิบเอ็ด

43 - sèe-sìp-săam
สี่สิบสาม

63 - hòk-sìp-săam
หกสิบสาม

88 - bpàaed-sìp-bpàaed
แปดสิบแปด

100 to infinity

100 to infinity

Thai has a word for each increment up to a million.

100 - nèung-róy
หนึ่งร้อย

1,000 - nèung-phan
หนึ่งพัน

10,000 - nèung-mèuun
หนึ่งหมื่น

100,000 - nèung-săaen
หนึ่งแสน

1,000,000 - nèung-láan
หนึ่งล้าน

10,000,000 - sìp-láan
สิบล้าน

100,000,000 - nèung-róy-láan
หนึ่งร้อยล้าน

1,000,000,000 - nèung-phan-láan
หนึ่งพันล้าน

For numbers in the order of one-hundred-and-something (1XX), Thai speakers will often drop the word *nèung*. For example, the number 120 might be read as *róy-yêe-sìp* rather than *nèung-róy-yêe-sìp.*

As you can see, counting in Thai is very logical. With a name for each increment, saying numbers is as easy as reading from left to right.

counting - putting it all together

House numbers

House numbers without a '/' between digits are read as either a regular number or individual digits. For example:

house number 156	*róy-hâa-sìp-hòk*
or	*nèung-hâa-hòk*

Condos, housing estates and villages almost always have a '/' (tháp) in between the numbers. The first number is the number for the entire condo or estate, and the second number is the individual condo unit or house. These numbers are read similarly, like this:

condo number 128/41	*nèung-sǎwng-bpàaed-tháp-sèe-sìp-èd*
or	*róy-yêe-sìp-bpàaed-tháp-sèe-sìp-èd*

Post codes are five digits throughout Thailand and are read as individual digits.

Phone numbers

Landlines and mobile numbers have differing amounts of digits, but both are spoken as individual numbers. When phone numbers are written or printed, Thais often separate them with hyphens to make them easier to read in chunks. These hyphens are not spoken; just say the numbers one by one, maybe with a pause where the hyphen would be.

081-370-0085
sŭun-bpàaed-nèung-săam-jèd-sŭun-sŭun-sŭun-bpàaed-hâa

Simple math

Let's learn the words for add, subtract, multiply, divide and equal to.

+	-	x	÷	=
bùuak	lóp	khuun	hăan (dûuai)	thâo-gàp

15 + 15 = 30
sìp-hâa bùuak sìp-hâa thâo-gàp săam-sìp
สิบห้าบวกสิบห้าเท่ากับสามสิบ

100 - 45 = 55
nèung-róy lóp sèe-sìp-hâa thâo-gàp hâa-sìp-hâa
หนึ่งร้อยลบสี่สิบห้าเท่ากับห้าสิบห้า

17 x 3 = 51
sìp-jèd khuun săam thâo-gàp hâa-sìp-èd
สิบเจ็ดคูณสามเท่ากับห้าสิบเอ็ด

0.9 ÷ 3 = 0.3
sŭun-jùd-gâo hăan dûuai săam thâo-gàp sŭun-jùd-săam
ศูนย์จุดเก้าหารด้วยสามเท่ากับศูนย์จุดสาม

1,000 + 3,200 = 4,200
nèung-phan bùuak săam-phan-săwng-róy thâo-gàp sèe-phan săwng-róy
หนึ่งพันบวกสามพันสองร้อยเท่ากับสี่พันสองร้อย

11,265 - 4,500 = 6,765
nèung-mèuun nèung-phan săwng-róy hòk-sìp-hâa lóp sèe-phan hâa-róy thâo-gàp hòk-phan jèd-róy hòk-sìp-hâa
หนึ่งหมื่นหนึ่งพันสองร้อยหกสิบห้าลบสี่พันห้าร้อยเท่ากับหกพันเจ็ดร้อยหกสิบห้า

155 x 40 = 6,200
nèung-róy hâa-sìp-hâa khuun sèe-sìp thâo-gàp hòk-phan săwng-róy
หนึ่งร้อยห้าสิบห้าคูณสี่สิบเท่ากับหกพันสองร้อย

120 ÷ 12 = 10
nèung-róy-yêe-sìp hăan dûuai sìp-săwng thâo-gàp sìp
หนึ่งร้อยยี่สิบหารด้วยสิบสองเท่ากับสิบ

500 + 600 = 1,100

hâa-róy bùuak hòk-róy thâo-gàp nèung-phan nèung-róy

ห้าร้อยบวกหกร้อยเท่ากับหนึ่งพันหนึ่งร้อย

0.65 x 6 = 3.9

sũun-jùd-hòk-hâa khuun hòk thâo-gàp sãam-jùd-gâo

ศูนย์จุดหกห้าคูณหกเท่ากับสามจุดเก้า

simple math

math quiz

Days of the week

days of the week

Sunday
wan-aa-thíd
วันอาทิตย์

Monday
wan-jan
วันจันทร์

Tuesday
wan-ang-khaan
วันอังคาร

Wednesday
wan-phúd
วันพุธ

Thursday
wan-phá-réu-hàd
วันพฤหัส

Friday
wan-sùk
วันศุกร์

Saturday
wan-sǎo
วันเสาร์

and finally ...

Always remember to add a polite particle to the end of your sentences. For men, add **khráp** at the end, and for ladies it's **khâ**. You'll find it encourages Thais to be more willing to speak with you.

be polite

Chapter 3

Personal pronouns

Thai uses the same personal pronouns for subject & object, so we only need to learn one word for each.

subject	object	subject & object	
I (masculine)	me	phŏm	ผม
I (feminine)	me	chăn	ฉัน
you	you	khun	คุณ
he	him	khăo	เขา
she	her	ther	เธอ
we	us	phûuak-rao	พวกเรา
they	them	phûuak-khăo	พวกเขา
it	it	man	มัน

personal pronouns

A quick grammar note: In a sentence, the 'subject' is typically a noun or pronoun, while the 'object' is the person or thing being acted upon by a 'verb'. For example:

subject	verb	object
He	loves	her.
She	loves	him.

Unlike English, the personal pronoun remains the same for both subject and object in Thai.

As a minimum, a sentence needs a subject and a verb.

As you're just beginning to learn Thai, the personal pronouns above are the safe word choices to use that will never offend anybody and are suitable in almost all situations. However, it's worth noting that these are not fixed. Thai has many more formal words and even more informal words. You will hear and learn these as you improve your conversation skills.

The only additional suggestion we would make at this point is that if you speak to children, don't use *khun*, use *ther* instead.

Another oddity you will certainly encounter is Thais referring to themselves in the third person by using their own name (or nickname). So someone with the nickname *Gûng* might say:

I'm tired. Gûng nèuuai กุ้งเหนื่อย	*instead of*	I'm tired. chăn nèuuai ฉันเหนื่อย

Likewise, you can use a person's name as a direct pronoun instead of 'you'. It may feel odd to address someone directly by their name, but it's useful if you're unsure which word the situation calls for.

Verbs 1

For those who left school some time ago and can't remember their verbs from nouns, verbs are the *action words* such as 'run' and 'sing'.

This book will introduce the most commonly used Thai verbs.

come maa มา	do, make tham ทำ	go bpai ไป
work tham-ngaan ทำงาน	drink dèuum ดื่ม	sleep nawn นอน
eat gin กิน	think khíd คิด	swim wâai-nám ว่ายน้ำ
look duu ดู	speak phûud พูด	read àan อ่าน
sit nâng นั่ง	write khĭian เขียน	to know rúu รู้ (a fact or information)

your first verbs

Appendix II lists the most commonly used Thai verbs.

Let's get started

Thai is spoken in the present simple tense, so if we just add a personal pronoun to a verb (subject + verb) we have a short but correct sentence. Look at the following examples:

I go.
phŏm bpai
ผมไป

She eats.
ther gin
เธอกิน

You come.
khun maa
คุณมา

We do.
phûuak-rao tham
พวกเราทำ

He drinks.
khăo dèuum
เขาดื่ม

They work.
phûuak-khăo tham-ngaan
พวกเขาทำงาน

your first sentences

It's normal to speak as simply as this, and context usually helps. There are no verb conjugations to deal with, and tense is achieved by context or by including a time indicator. So all of the following are correct, but can be said in a more precise way when necessary.

I go.
phŏm bpai
ผมไป

I went.
phŏm bpai
ผมไป

I will go.
phŏm bpai
ผมไป

I am going.
phŏm bpai
ผมไป

exercise 1

Verbs 2

like
châwp
ชอบ

remember
jam
จำ

love
rák
รัก

see
hĕn
เห็น

understand
khâo-jai
เข้าใจ

hear
dâi-yin
ได้ยิน

call (phone)
thoo-hăa
โทรหา

listen
fang
ฟัง

wait
raw
รอ

to know (a person or place)
rúu-jàk
รู้จัก

more verbs

These new verbs allow us to add an object to the sentence, like this:

subject	**verb**	**object**
I	like	**you**.
phŏm	châwp	**khun**
ผม	ชอบ	คุณ

I love you.
phŏm rák khun
ผมรักคุณ

He understands me.
khăo khâo-jai chăn
เขาเข้าใจฉัน

She remembers me.
ther jam phŏm
เธอจำผม

I hear(d) you.
chăn dâi-yin khun
ฉันได้ยินคุณ

I go to Karon.
phŏm bpai Karon
ผมไปกะรน

He knows us.
khăo rúu-jàk phûuak-rao
เขารู้จักพวกเรา

You call her.
khun thoo-hăa ther
คุณโทรหาเธอ

We see it.
phûuak-rao hĕn man
พวกเราเห็นมัน

I listen to you.
phŏm fang khun
ผมฟังคุณ

You come to Phuket.
khun maa phuu-gèd
คุณมาภูเก็ต

And we can mix it up a bit by using names or two verbs, like this:

Peter likes **Jane**.
Peter châwp **Jane**
ปีเตอร์ชอบเจน

Jane loves me.
Jane rák phŏm
เจนรักผม

Jane calls him.
Jane thoo-hăa khăo
เจนโทรหาเขา

Listen to me.
fang chăn
ฟังฉัน

I heard.
phŏm dâi-yin
ผมได้ยิน

Peter knows Jane.
Peter rúu-jàk Jane
ปีเตอร์รู้จักเจน

Jane **likes** pizza.
Jane **châwp** phíd-sâa
เจนชอบพิซซ่า

Jane **likes** to **eat** pizza.
Jane **châwp gin** phíd-sâa
เจนชอบกินพิซซ่า

Peter likes beer.
Peter châwp biia
ปีเตอร์ชอบเบียร์

Peter likes to drink beer.
Peter châwp dèuum biia
ปีเตอร์ชอบดื่มเบียร์

We like to swim.
phûuak-rao châwp wâai-nám
พวกเราชอบว่ายน้ำ

She likes to read.
ther châwp àan
เธอชอบอ่าน

As you can see, with just the pronouns and a few verbs it's already possible to make some simple sentences. Watch the video and listen to the audio online, then try making up your own new sentences from the vocabulary you now have. Finally, have a go at completing the online exercise yourself.

building on our sentences   exercise 2

Want to, would like to

want to ...
dtâwng-gaan
ต้องการ

would like to ...
yàak (jà)
อยาก(จะ)

These are both 'helping verbs' that go in front of another verb. We can include *dtâwng-gaan* in our sentences like this:

I **want to** go.
chăn **dtâwng-gaan** bpai
ฉันต้องการไป

You want to speak.
khun dtâwng-gaan phûud
คุณต้องการพูด

He wants to see.
khăo dtâwng-gaan hĕn
เขาต้องการเห็น

I want to sit.
phŏm dtâwng-gaan nâng
ผมต้องการนั่ง

Jane wants to read.
Jane dtâwng-gaan àan
เจนต้องการอ่าน

Peter wants to come.
Peter dtâwng-gaan maa
ปีเตอร์ต้องการมา

He wants to swim.
khăo dtâwng-gaan wâai-nám
เขาต้องการว่ายน้ำ

It wants to go.
man dtâwng-gaan bpai
มันต้องการไป

yàak-jà or just *yàak* can be used directly in place of *dtâwng-gaan*:

I **would like to** go.
chăn **yàak-jà** bpai
ฉันอยากจะไป

You would like to see.
khun yàak hĕn
คุณอยากเห็น

He would like to sit.
khăo yàak-jà nâng
เขาอยากจะนั่ง

She would like to come.
ther yàak maa
เธออยากมา

Jane would like to eat pizza.
Jane yàak-jà gin phíd-sâa
เจนอยากจะกินพิซซ่า

Peter would like to drink beer.
Peter yàak dèuum biia
ปีเตอร์อยากดื่มเบียร์

The meaning is subtly different between 'want to' and 'would like to', just as it is in English.

want to & would like to

exercise 3

Here & There

here	there
thêe-nêe	thêe-nân
ที่นี่	ที่นั่น

Here and *there* are the most common adverbs of place. They always follow the verb in a sentence.

I want to wait **here**.
chăn dtâwng-gaan raw **thêe-nêe**
ฉันต้องการรอที่นี่

Peter wants to go **there**.
Peter dtâwng-gaan bpai **thêe-nân**
ปีเตอร์ต้องการไปที่นั่น

He wants to sit here.
khăo dtâwng-gaan nâng thêe-nêe
เขาต้องการนั่งที่นี่

Jane wants to wait here.
Jane dtâwng-gaan raw thêe-nêe
เจนต้องการรอที่นี่

We would like to swim there.
phûuak-rao yàak-jà wâai-nám thêe-nân
พวกเราอยากจะว่ายน้ำที่นั่น

They want to sleep here.
phûuak-khăo dtâwng-gaan nawn thêe-nêe
พวกเขาต้องการนอนที่นี่

here and there

exercise 4

Travelling verbs

walk
dern
เดิน

run
wîng
วิ่ง

fly
bin
บิน

drive (a car)
khàp ród-yon
ขับ (รถยนต์)

ride (a motorcycle)
khèe ród-maw-ther-sai
ขี่ (รถมอเตอร์ไซค์)

take a train
nâng ród-fai
นั่งรถไฟ

These travelling verbs are always used with come (*maa*) or go (*bpai*) when there is a starting-point or destination.

We use *bpai* when the action is moving away from the speaker, and *maa* when it is coming toward the speaker.

I walk.
chăn dern
ฉันเดิน

I walked here.
chăn dern **maa** thêe-nêe
ฉันเดินมาที่นี่

He drives to Phuket.
khǎo khàp ród **bpai** phuu-gèd[1]
เขาขับรถไปภูเก็ต

Jane likes to run.
Jane châwp wîng
เจนชอบวิ่ง

She ran to Karon.
ther wîng **bpai** Karon
เธอวิ่งไปกะรน

We fly (flew) to Chiang Mai.
phûuak-rao bin bpai Chiang Mai
พวกเราบินไปเชียงใหม่

I took a train to Bangkok.
phǒm nâng ród-fai bpai grung-thâep[2]
ผมนั่งรถไฟไปกรุงเทพ

He rode to Kamala.
khǎo khèe maw-ther-sai bpai Kamala[3]
เขาขี่มอเตอร์ไซค์ไปกมลา

1. *ród-yon* usually drops the *yon,* as in the example.
2. Thais never call their capital Bangkok. In Thai it is known as *grung-thâep,* City of Angels.
3. *ród-maw-ther-sai* usually drops the *ród,* as in the example.

travelling verbs

exercise 5

Negatives

no, not, do not, does not
mâi
ไม่

This couldn't be easier, as this one word in Thai allows us to say all of these. The sentence form is subject + *mâi* + verb.

I **don't go**.
phǒm **mâi bpai**
ผมไม่ไป

You **don't eat**.
khun **mâi gin**
คุณไม่กิน

He doesn't like me.
khăo mâi châwp chăn
เขาไม่ชอบฉัน

You don't know.
khun mâi rúu
คุณไม่รู้

We don't sit here.
rao mâi nâng thêe-nêe
เราไม่นั่งที่นี่

He doesn't understand you.
khăo mâi khâo-jai khun
เขาไม่เข้าใจคุณ

I don't understand.
chăn mâi khâo-jai
ฉันไม่เข้าใจ

She doesn't know Peter.
ther mâi rúu-jàk Peter
เธอไม่รู้จักปีเตอร์

I don't like you.
phŏm mâi châwp khun
ผมไม่ชอบคุณ

We don't walk to Karon.
phûuak-rao mâi dern bpai Karon
พวกเราไม่เดินไปกะรน

I don't like working here.
chăn mâi châwp tham-ngaan thêe-nêe
ฉันไม่ชอบทำงานที่นี่

Remember that *want to* and *would like to* are also verbs, so *mâi* always comes before them too, when they are present.

I **don't want to** go.
phŏm **mâi dtâwng-gaan** bpai
ผมไม่ต้องการไป

You don't want to eat.
khun mâi dtâwng-gaan gin
คุณไม่ต้องการกิน

He doesn't want to sit here.
khăo mâi dtâwng-gaan nâng thêe-nêe
เขาไม่ต้องการนั่งที่นี่

I **wouldn't like to** go there.
chăn **mâi yàak-jà** bpai thêe-nân
ฉันไม่อยากจะไปที่นั่น

I wouldn't like to work here.
chăn mâi yàak-jà tham-ngaan thêe-nêe
ฉันไม่อยากจะทำงานที่นี่

They don't want to swim there.
phûuak-khăo mâi dtâwng-gaan wâai-nám thêe-nân
พวกเขาไม่ต้องการว่ายน้ำที่นั่น

negatives   exercise 6

Conjunctions

Conjunctions, or connecting words, function in the same way as in English and many other languages. They connect two parts of a sentence together, with a different effect depending on the word used. Conjunctions help us make longer sentences very easily.

with

---

with
gàp
กับ

The sentence form is: 1st person + verb + *gàp* + 2nd person
or 2nd person + verb + *gàp* + 3rd person

Our first conjunction we'll use with people, as in these examples (including negatives):

I go **with you**.
chăn bpai **gàp khun**
ฉันไปกับคุณ

You come **with me**.
khun maa **gàp chăn**
คุณมากับฉัน

He goes to swim with them.
khăo bpai wâai-nám gàp phûuak-khăo
เขาไปว่ายน้ำกับพวกเขา

I want to sit here with you.
phŏm dtâwng-gaan nâng thêe-nêe gàp khun
ผมต้องการนั่งที่นี่กับคุณ

You go there with Peter.
khun bpai thêe-nân gàp Peter
คุณไปที่นั่นกับปีเตอร์

She did it with them.
ther tham gàp phûuak-khăo
เธอทำกับพวกเขา

I don't go with you.
phŏm mâi bpai gàp khun
ผมไม่ไปกับคุณ

You don't go there with me.
khun mâi bpai thêe-nân gàp phŏm
คุณไม่ไปที่นั่นกับผม

Peter doesn't go with Jane.
Peter mâi bpai gàp Jane
ปีเตอร์ไม่ไปกับเจน

I don't want to sit here with them.
chăn mâi dtâwng-gaan nâng thêe-nêe gàp phûuak-khăo
ฉันไม่ต้องการนั่งที่นี่กับพวกเขา

and

---

and
láe
และ

We use the conjunction *láe* to add or include, such as 'knife and fork' or 'Peter and Jane'. We'll use it later with nouns, but for now we'll practise with our pronouns.

You **and me**.
khun **láe chăn**
คุณและฉัน

Peter and Jane go to Phuket.
Peter láe Jane bpai phuu-gèd
ปีเตอร์และเจนไปภูเก็ต

He and she sit here.
khăo láe ther nâng thêe-nêe
เขาและเธอนั่งที่นี่

You and I eat there.
khun láe chăn gin thêe-nân
คุณและฉันกินที่นั่น

You and me and Peter.
khun láe phŏm láe Peter
คุณและผมและปีเตอร์

You **and** I go to Phuket **with** Jane.
khun **láe** chăn bpai phuu-gèd **gàp** Jane
คุณและฉันไปภูเก็ตกับเจน

two conjunctions — exercise 7

Future tense

will
jà
จะ

We use the word *jà* to indicate future tense; that something will take place in the future. Later we'll add a time indicator to say *when* in the future it will happen.

In positive sentences the form is:

subject + *jà* + verb

And in negative sentences is:

subject + *jà* + *mâi* + verb

You **will** eat.
khun **jà** gin
คุณจะกิน

I will go there.
phŏm jà bpai thêe-nân
ผมจะไปที่นั่น

He **will not** like me.
khăo **jà mâi** châwp chăn
เขาจะไม่ชอบฉัน

I will go with you.
chăn jà bpai gàp khun
ฉันจะไปกับคุณ

I will understand.
chăn jà khâo-jai
ฉันจะเข้าใจ

You will not go there.
khun jà mâi bpai thêe-nân
คุณจะไม่ไปที่นั่น

We will not sit here.
rao jà mâi nâng thêe-nêe
เราจะไม่นั่งที่นี่

He will go to Phuket.
khăo jà bpai phuu-gèd
เขาจะไปภูเก็ต

He will not want to go there.
khăo jà mâi dtâwng-gaan bpai thêe-nân
เขาจะไม่ต้องการไปที่นั่น

I don't like him, I will not speak with him.
chăn mâi châwp khăo, chăn jà mâi phûud gàp khăo
ฉันไม่ชอบเขา ฉันจะไม่พูดกับเขา

future tense exercise 8

Questions

asking questions

......?
... măi?
... ไหม

You already know how to make sentences as positive statements, so making questions is the easiest thing ever. Questions are formed in exactly the same way as we make a positive statement – all we do is add the question word *măi* at the end. Yes, that's all there is to it!

The sentence form is subject + verb + *măi*. Any other content in the sentence must come before the question word, as in the following example constructions:

Do you ......?
khun ...... mǎi?
คุณ ......ไหม

Does he/she ......?
khǎo/ther ...... mǎi?
เขา/เธอ ...... ไหม

Do you want to ......?
khun dtâwng-gaan ...... mǎi?
คุณต้องการ ...... ไหม

Would you like to ......?
khun yàak-jà ...... mǎi?
คุณอยากจะ ...... ไหม

Will you ......?
khun jà ...... mǎi?
คุณจะ ...... ไหม

Here are some example sentences:

Do you understand**?**
khun khâo-jai **mǎi?**
คุณเข้าใจไหม

Does he like Phuket**?**
khǎo châwp phuu-gèd **mǎi?**
เขาชอบภูเก็ตไหม

Does she want to swim?
ther dtâwng-gaan wâai-nám mǎi?
เธอต้องการว่ายน้ำไหม

Will he go with us**?**
khǎo **jà** bpai gàp phûuak-rao **mǎi?**
เขาจะไปกับพวกเราไหม

Will you wait here?
khun jà raw thêe-nêe mǎi?
คุณจะรอที่นี่ไหม

Do you like working here?
khun châwp tham-ngaan thêe-nêe mǎi?
คุณชอบทำงานที่นี่ไหม

Would you like to come with us**?**
khun yàak-jà maa gàp phûuak-rao **mǎi?**
คุณอยากจะมากับพวกเราไหม

asking questions

answering questions

Questions using a verb (which is all we have learned so far) are answered by repeating the verb on its own for a positive answer, or the verb preceded by the word *mâi* for a negative answer.

Question	Yes	No
khun rúu mǎi? คุณรู้ไหม	rúu รู้	mâi rúu ไม่รู้
ther khâo-jai mǎi? เธอเข้าใจไหม	khâo-jai เข้าใจ	mâi khâo-jai ไม่เข้าใจ
phûuak-khǎo rúu-jàk Peter mǎi? พวกเขารู้จักปีเตอร์ไหม	rúu-jàk รู้จัก	mâi rúu-jàk ไม่รู้จัก
khun dtâwng-gaan gin mǎi? คุณต้องการกินไหม	dtâwng-gaan ต้องการ	mâi dtâwng-gaan ไม่ต้องการ

In the final example there are two more possible answers because there are two verbs in the sentence. It can also be answered like this:

Question	Yes	No
khun dtâwng-gaan gin mǎi? คุณต้องการกินไหม	gin กิน	mâi gin ไม่กิน
khun dtâwng-gaan gin mǎi? คุณต้องการกินไหม	dtâwng-gaan gin ต้องการกิน	mâi dtâwng-gaan gin ไม่ต้องการกิน

short question form

Questions may be asked in a shorter form if you are speaking to someone directly. In this case you can drop the *khun* and just use the verb with *mǎi*. Answering is the same:

Question	Yes	No
rúu mǎi? รู้ไหม	rúu รู้	mâi rúu ไม่รู้
khâo-jai mǎi? เข้าใจไหม	khâo-jai เข้าใจ	mâi khâo-jai ไม่เข้าใจ

rúu-jàk Peter măi? รู้จักปีเตอร์ไหม	rúu-jàk รู้จัก	mâi rúu-jàk ไม่รู้จัก
dtâwng-gaan gin thêe-nêe măi? ต้องการกินที่นี่ไหม	dtâwng-gaan ต้องการ	mâi dtâwng-gaan ไม่ต้องการ
châwp phuu-gèd măi? ชอบภูเก็ตไหม	châwp ชอบ	mâi châwp ไม่ชอบ

exercise 9

chapter 3 quiz

Chapter 4

New vocabulary

We'll introduce a couple of new words here which will prove useful in conversation.

language
phaa-sǎa
ภาษา

Thai language
phaa-sǎa thai
ภาษาไทย

English language
phaa-sǎa ang-grìd
ภาษาอังกฤษ

Ability

can

---

can
dâi
ได้

The word dâi is used to express the ability to do something. It is always added at the end of a sentence in the form subject + verb + *dâi* as in these examples:

I **can** go.
phǒm bpai **dâi**
ผมไปได้

She **can** come.
ther maa **dâi**
เธอมาได้

I can speak English.
chǎn phûud phaa-sǎa ang-grìd dâi
ฉันพูดภาษาอังกฤษได้

Peter can speak Thai.
Peter phûud phaa-sǎa thai dâi
ปีเตอร์พูดภาษาไทยได้

You can eat with us.
khun gin gàp phûuak-rao dâi
คุณกินกับพวกเราได้

I can do it.
phŏm tham dâi
ผมทำได้

He can sit with us.
khăo nâng gàp phûuak-rao dâi
เขานั่งกับพวกเราได้

can   exercise 10

cannot

---

can't
mâi-dâi
ไม่ได้

This is exactly the same as above except that we add the negative word *mâi* in front of *dâi* to say cannot. The format is subject + verb + *mâi-dâi*. We'll use the same examples as above:

I **can't** go.
phŏm bpai **mâi-dâi**
ผมไปไม่ได้

She **can't** come.
ther maa **mâi-dâi**
เธอมาไม่ได้

I can't speak English.
chăn phûud phaa-săa ang-grìd mâi-dâi
ฉันพูดภาษาอังกฤษไม่ได้

Peter can't speak Thai.
Peter phûud phaa-săa thai mâi-dâi
ปีเตอร์พูดภาษาไทยไม่ได้

You can't eat with us.
khun gin gàp phûuak-rao mâi-dâi
คุณกินกับพวกเราไม่ได้

I can't do it.
phŏm tham mâi-dâi
ผมทำไม่ได้

He can't sit with us.
khăo nâng gàp phûuak-rao mâi-dâi
เขานั่งกับพวกเราไม่ได้

cannot   exercise 11

Can?

Can ......?
...... dâi măi?
......ได้ไหม

Once again the format is the same, except that we add the question word *măi*? after *dâi*. In this case it is subject + verb + *dâi măi*? Again, using the same examples:

Can I go**?**
phŏm bpai **dâi măi?**
ผมไปได้ไหม

Can she come**?**
ther maa **dâi măi?**
เธอมาได้ไหม

Can I speak English?
chăn phûud phaa-săa ang-grìd dâi măi?
ฉันพูดภาษาอังกฤษได้ไหม

Can Peter speak Thai?
Peter phûud phaa-săa thai dâi măi?
ปีเตอร์พูดภาษาไทยได้ไหม

Can you eat with us?
khun gin gàp phûuak-rao dâi măi?
คุณกินกับพวกเราได้ไหม

Can I do it?
phŏm tham dâi măi?
ผมทำได้ไหม

Can he sit with us?
khăo nâng gàp phûuak-rao dâi măi?
เขานั่งกับพวกเราได้ไหม

answering 'can?' questions

dâi măi? questions are answered using either *dâi* or *mâi-dâi*.

Question	Yes	No
phŏm bpai dâi măi? ผมไปได้ไหม	dâi ได้	mâi-dâi ไม่ได้
ther raw dâi măi? เธอรอได้ไหม	dâi ได้	mâi-dâi ไม่ได้
khun gin thêe-nêe dâi măi? คุณกินที่นี่ได้ไหม	dâi ได้	mâi-dâi ไม่ได้
khăo maa phuu-gèd dâi măi? เขามาภูเก็ตได้ไหม	dâi ได้	mâi-dâi ไม่ได้

It is also acceptable to include the verb along with *dâi* or *mâi-dâi*.

Question	Yes	No
phŏm bpai dâi măi? ผมไปได้ไหม	bpai dâi ไปได้	bpai mâi-dâi ไปไม่ได้
ther raw dâi măi? เธอรอได้ไหม	raw dâi รอได้	raw mâi-dâi รอไม่ได้
khun gin thêe-nêe dâi măi? คุณกินที่นี่ได้ไหม	gin dâi กินได้	gin mâi-dâi กินไม่ได้
khăo maa phuu-gèd dâi măi? เขามาภูเก็ตได้ไหม	maa dâi มาได้	maa mâi-dâi มาไม่ได้

can? questions & answers — exercise 12

some exceptions

There are a number of exceptions using *dâi* with some verbs. The following are from the vocabulary we have learned so far. Exceptions always use a pair of words.

verb	literal meaning	can	cannot
nawn นอน	lay down	nawn-làp นอนหลับ	nawn mâi làp นอนไม่หลับ

hĕn เห็น	see	mawng-hĕn มองเห็น	mawng mâi hĕn มองไม่เห็น
khíd คิด	think	khíd-àwk คิดออก	khíd mâi àwk คิดไม่ออก

Note that the negative is formed by placing *mâi* between the pair of words.

To understand the construction above we need to know the meaning of the new words used in the pairs:

sleep làp หลับ	look mawng มอง	come out, exit àwk ออก

If we look at the literal meaning of the expressions it will become easier to understand.

can	**literal meaning**	**actual meaning**
nawn-làp	lay down and sleep	to sleep
mawng-hĕn	look and see	to see
khíd-àwk	think and come out	to know the answer
cannot	**literal meaning**	**actual meaning**
nawn mâi làp	lay down, but not sleep	cannot sleep
mawng mâi hĕn	look, but not see	cannot see
khíd mâi àwk	think, but not come out	don't know

We ask questions in a similar way:

verb	**question**	**yes**	**no**
nawn นอน	khun nawn-làp măi? คุณนอนหลับไหม	nawn-làp นอนหลับ	nawn mâi làp นอนไม่หลับ
hĕn เห็น	khăo mawng-hĕn măi? เขามองเห็นไหม	mawng-hĕn มองเห็น	mawng mâi hĕn มองไม่เห็น
khíd คิด	ther khíd àwk măi? เธอคิดออกไหม	khíd-àwk คิดออก	khíd mâi àwk คิดไม่ออก

You will come across more of these exceptions as you learn new vocabulary.

cannot (irregular)

chapter 4 quiz

Chapter 5

Greetings & Small talk

Now that we can make sentences, ask questions and respond, we are able to converse at least a little in Thai. Before we can go out to practise though, we need to know how to greet people and make some small talk.

Hello/Goodbye.
sà-wàd-dee
สวัสดี

Good night.
raa-dtree-sà-wàd
ราตรีสวัสดิ์

How are you?
khun sà-baai dee mǎi?
คุณสบายดีไหม

Thank you.
khàwp khun
ขอบคุณ

Just a moment.
raw sák-khrûu
รอสักครู่

Come quickly!
maa rew-rew
มาเร็ว ๆ !

Never mind./That's alright.
mâi bpen rai
ไม่เป็นไร

He has a cold.
khǎo bpen wàd
เขาเป็นหวัด

I am very busy.
phǒm yûng mâak
ผมยุ่งมาก

Pleased to meet you.
yin-dee thêe dâi rúu-jàk
ยินดีที่ได้รู้จัก

Goodbye/farewell.
laa gàwn
ลาก่อน

I am fine./I am well.
phǒm sà-baai dee
ผมสบายดี

Excuse me./Sorry.
khǎw thôod (general use)
ขอโทษ

What did you say?
khun phûud à-rai?
คุณพูดอะไร?

Go slowly!
bpai cháa-cháa
ไปช้า ๆ !

You're welcome.
yin-dee
ยินดี

I have a headache.
phǒm bpùuad hǔua
ผมปวดหัว

To arrive late.
maa sǎai
มาสาย

Please come in.
chern khâang-nai
เชิญข้างใน

How much is it?
raa-khaa thâo-rài?
ราคาเท่าไหร่

See you tomorrow.
phóp gan phrûng-née
พบกันพรุ่งนี้

See you again.
phóp gan mài
พบกันใหม่

I am sorry.
phŏm sĭia-jai (to express regret)
ผมเสียใจ

What time is it?
waeh-laa thâo-rài/gèe moong láeo
เวลาเท่าไหร่/กี่โมงแล้ว

I've forgotten.
phŏm leuum láeo
ผมลืมแล้ว

I don't agree.
phŏm mâi hĕn dûuai
ผมไม่เห็นด้วย

See you later.
dĭaao phóp gan
เดี๋ยวพบกัน

No problem.
mâi mee bpan-hăa
ไม่มีปัญหา

common expressions

Chapter 6

New vocabulary

nouns

These nouns are all objects, so that we can learn to describe them, count them, and say who owns them. Nouns as places will come later when we learn the verb-to-be and 'where' questions.

furniture

table
dtóe
โต๊ะ

fridge
dtûu-yen
ตู้เย็น

wardrobe
dtûu-sêuua-phâa
ตู้เสื้อผ้า

chair
gâo-êe
เก้าอี้

sofa
soo-faa
โซฟา

food & drink

plate
jaan
จาน

glass
gâaeo
แก้ว

spoon
cháwn
ช้อน

cup
thûuai
ถ้วย

fork
sâwm
ส้อม

knife
mêed
มีด

food
aa-hăan
อาหาร

water
nám
น้ำ

kettle
gaa-dtôm-nám-ráwn
กาต้มน้ำร้อน

microwave
mai-khroo-wâeb
ไมโครเวฟ

clothing

shirt/blouse
sêuua
เสื้อ

T-shirt
sêuua-yêuud
เสื้อยืด

denim jeans
gaang-gaeng-yeen
กางเกงยีนส์

handbag grà-bpăo กระเป๋า	shorts gaang-gaeng-khăa-sân กางเกงขาสั้น	
hat mùuak หมวก	skirt grà-bproong กระโปรง	umbrella rôm ร่ม

technology

smartphone meuu-thĕuu มือถือ	remote control ree-mòed รีโมท	tablet tháaeb-lèd แท็บเล็ต
notebook nóed-búk โน๊ตบุ๊ค	TV thee-wee ทีวี	air-con aae แอร์
fan phád-lom พัดลม	computer khawm-piw-dtêr คอมพิวเตอร์	

miscellaneous

door bprà-dtuu ประตู	window nâa-dtàang หน้าต่าง

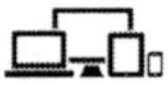 nouns

Appendix III lists the most commonly used Thai nouns.

adjectives

In opposite pairs (mostly).

small lék เล็ก	big/large yài ใหญ่
shut/closed/off bpìd ปิด	open/on bpèrd เปิด
light weight bao เบา	heavy weight nàk หนัก

clean sà-àad สะอาด	dirty sòk-gà-bpròk สกปรก
long yaao ยาว	short sân สั้น
wide gwâang กว้าง	narrow khâaep แคบ
full dtem เต็ม	empty bplào เปล่า
high/tall sǔung สูง	low (height) dtîia เตี้ย
sharp (pointed) lǎaem แหลม	sharp (blade) khom คม
new mài ใหม่	old (object) gào เก่า
old (person, animal) gàae แก่	warm, to warm ùn[1] อุ่น
hot ráwn ร้อน	cold (objects) yen เย็น

1. *ùn* is also a verb meaning 'to warm', as in 'warm the plate'.

colours

colour
sěe
สี

black
sěe-dam
สีดำ

white
sěe-khăao
สีขาว

yellow
sěe-lěuuang
สีเหลือง

green
sěe-khĭaao
สีเขียว

red
sěe-daaeng
สีแดง

grey
sěe-thao
สีเทา

light blue
sěe-fáa
สีฟ้า

dark blue
sěe-nám-ngern
สีน้ำเงิน

adjectives

Appendix IV lists the most commonly used Thai adjectives.

Using adjectives

Adjectives always follow the noun that they are describing, as in these examples.

a **small** table
dtóe **lék**
โต๊ะเล็ก

a **long** sofa
soo-faa **yaao**
โซฟายาว

a sharp knife
mêed khom
มีดคม

a heavy kettle
gaa-dtôm-nám-ráwn nàk
กาต้มน้ำร้อนหนัก

hot food
aa-hăan ráwn
อาหารร้อน

an old T-shirt
sêuua-yêuud gào
เสื้อยืดเก่า

a short skirt
grà-bproong sân
กระโปรงสั้น

a cold air-con
aae yen
แอร์เย็น

a new mobile phone
meuu-thěuu mài
มือถือใหม่

a wide door
bprà-dtuu gwâang
ประตูกว้าง

a tall window
nâa-dtàang sŭung
หน้าต่างสูง

a fast, black car
ród-yon sěe-dam, rew
รถยนต์สีดำเร็ว

a dirty, red motorcycle
rót-maw-ther-sai sěe-daaeng, sòk-gà-bpròk
รถมอเตอร์ไซค์สีแดงสกปรก

describing objects — exercise 13

Adjectives as verbs

Open and close, turn on and off, switch on and off, are both adjectives and verbs. For example, you can 'open a door' (verb) or the 'door is open' (an open door – adjective). The only difference is in the word order; as a verb they come before the noun. Let's look at the difference:

as adjectives	**as verbs**
an **open** door bprà-dtuu **bpèrd** ประตูเปิด	**open** the door **bpèrd** bprà-dtuu เปิดประตู
a closed window nâa-dtàang bpìd หน้าต่างปิด	close the window bpìd nâa-dtàang ปิดหน้าต่าง
the TV is on thee-wee bpèrd ทีวีเปิด	turn on the TV bpèrd thee-wee เปิดทีวี
the fan is off phád-lom bpìd พัดลมปิด	switch off the fan bpìd phád-lom ปิดพัดลม

The fridge is open, close the fridge door.
dtûu-yen bpèrd, bpìd bprà-dtuu dtûu-yen
ตู้เย็นเปิด ปิดประตูตู้เย็น

The air-con is on and the window is open, close the window.
aae bpèrd láe nâa-dtàang bpèrd, bpìd nâa-dtàang
แอร์เปิดและหน้าต่างเปิด ปิดหน้าต่าง

It's hot. You close the door and window. I will switch on the fan and the air-con.

man ráwn. khun bpìd bprà-dtuu láe nâa-dtàang. phŏm jà bpèrd phád-lom láe aae

มันร้อน คุณปิดประตูและหน้าต่าง ผมจะเปิดพัดลมและแอร์

adjective or verb?

exercise 14

chapter 6 quiz

Chapter 7

This & That

this (these)	that (those)
nêe	nân
นี่	นั่น

These words are pronouns and are both falling tone. From page 62 you will see similar words used as modifiers, which are high tone.

Verb-to-be 1

is, am, are
bpen
เป็น

There are three verbs-to-be in Thai. This first one is used with objects (everything except people).

Possessives

my/mine
khăwng-phŏm/chăn
ของผม/ฉัน

your/yours
khăwng-khun
ของคุณ

his
khăwng-khăo
ของเขา

her/hers
khăwng-ther
ของเธอ

our/ours
khăwng-phûuak-rao
ของพวกเรา

their/theirs
khăwng-phûuak-khăo
ของพวกเขา

its
khăwng-man
ของมัน

Peter's
khăwng-Peter
ของปีเตอร์

possessive adjectives

Possessive adjectives come before a pronoun to show who or what owns it. It is simply the addition of the word *khăwng* in front of the pronoun.

my chair
gâo-êe **khǎwng-phǒm**
เก้าอี้ของผม

your plate
jaan **khǎwng-khun**
จานของคุณ

our car
ród-yon khǎwng-phûuak-rao
รถยนต์ของพวกเรา

Jane's yellow blouse
sêuua sěe-lěuuang khǎwng-Jane
เสื้อสีเหลืองของเจน

possessive adjectives

Just as *phûuak-rao* is often abbreviated to *rao*, and *ród-yon* is shortened to *ród*, Thai speakers will often drop the possessive *khǎwng*, like this:

my chair
gâo-êe phǒm
เก้าอี้ผม

your plate
jaan khun
จานคุณ

our car
ród rao
รถเรา

possessive pronouns

Now let's look at examples with the verb-to-be included. These are called possessive pronouns, as they replace the pronoun in the sentence. Unlike English, they still use the same word, *khǎwng*.

This is **mine**.
nêe bpen **khǎwng-chǎn**
นี่เป็นของฉัน

This is yours.
nêe bpen khǎwng-khun
นี่เป็นของคุณ

That is my chair.
nân bpen gâo-êe khǎwng-phǒm
นั่นเป็นเก้าอี้ของผม

That is her motorcycle.
nân bpen ród maw-ther-sai khǎwng-ther
นั่นเป็นรถมอเตอร์ไซค์ของเธอ

That is Peter's new notebook.
nân bpen nóed-búk mài khăwng-Peter
นั่นเป็นโน้ตบุ๊กใหม่ของปีเตอร์

This is my glass and that is yours.
nêe bpen gâaeo khăwng-chăn láe nân bpen gâaeo khăwng-khun
นี่เป็นแก้วของฉันและนั่นเป็นแก้วของคุณ

verb-to-be, this & that exercise 15

Who

who
khrai
ใคร

Most question words come at the end of the sentence in Thai, but *khrai* mostly comes at the beginning.

Who will go with you?
khrai jà bpai gàp khun?
ใครจะไปกับคุณ

Who will you go with?
khun jà bpai gàp **khrai**?
คุณจะไปกับใคร

Who is Peter talking to?
Peter phûud gàp khrai?
ปีเตอร์พูดกับใคร

Who is sitting here?
khrai nâng thêe-nêe?
ใครนั่งที่นี่

Who would like to swim with me?
khrai yàak-jà wâai-nám gàp chăn?
ใครอยากจะว่ายน้ำกับฉัน

Who can come?
khrai maa dâi?
ใครมาได้

Whose

whose
khǎwng-khrai
ของใคร

'Whose' is made up of the possessive word (*khǎwng*) and who (*khrai*). *khǎwng-khrai* is placed after the noun to query ownership.

Whose handbag is this?
nêe bpen grà-bpǎo **khǎwng-khrai**?
นี่เป็นกระเป๋าของใคร

Whose chair is that?
nân bpen gâo-êe khǎwng-khrai?
นั่นเป็นเก้าอี้ของใคร

This is mine, whose is that?
nêe bpen khǎwng-chǎn, nân bpen khǎwng-khrai?
นี่เป็นของฉัน นั่นเป็นของใคร

who & whose

exercise 16

chapter 7 quiz

Chapter 8

Verb-to-be 2

is, am, are	at
yùu	thêe
อยู่	ที่

We use *yùu* along with the preposition *thêe* to say *is at ..., am at ..., are at ...*

This second verb-to-be is used exclusively with location, so first we need some places.

New vocabulary

places

7-11 sae-wên เซเว่น	Central sen-thrân เซ็นทรัล	Jungceylon jang-see-lawn จังซีลอน
bank thá-naa-khaan ธนาคาร	house, home bâan บ้าน	airport sà-năam-bin สนามบิน
shop ráan ร้าน	embassy sà-thăan-thûud สถานทูต	district office am-pher อำเภอ
school roong-riian โรงเรียน	post office bprai-sà-nee ไปรษณีย์	market dtà-làad ตลาด
restaurant ráan-aa-hăan ร้านอาหาร	hotel roong-raaem โรงแรม	cinema roong-năng โรงหนัง
village mùu-bâan หมู่บ้าน	bar baa บาร์	coffee shop ráan-gaa-faae ร้านกาแฟ

police station sà-thăa-nee dtam-rùuad สถานีตำรวจ	railway station sà-thăa-nee ród-fai สถานีรถไฟ

hospital
roong-phá-yaa-baan
โรงพยาบาล

places

Appendix VI lists some common placenames.

verbs

buy séuu ซื้อ	sell khăai ขาย

Let's look at some examples of the verb-to-be *yùu*:

I **am at** home.
chăn **yùu thêe** bâan
ฉันอยู่ที่บ้าน

He **is at** school.
khăo **yùu thêe** roong-riian
เขาอยู่ที่โรงเรียน

She **is not at** the shop.
ther **mâi yùu thêe** ráan
เธอไม่อยู่ที่ร้าน

We are at the cinema.
phûuak-rao yùu thêe roong-năng
พวกเราอยู่ที่โรงหนัง

Peter is at the restaurant with Jane.
Peter yùu thêe ráan-aa-hăan gàp Jane
ปีเตอร์อยู่ที่ร้านอาหารกับเจน

He's not here, he went to the bar.
khăo mâi yùu thêe-nêe, khăo bpai baa
เขาไม่อยู่ที่นี่ เขาไปบาร์

verb-to-be 2

exercise 17

Where

where?
thêe-nǎi?
ที่ไหน

The question word *thêe-nǎi* comes at the end of a sentence.

When used with verbs **other than** *yùu*, the format is:

subject + verb + *thêe-nǎi?*

When used with **nouns** the format is:

place/object + *yùu* + *thêe-nǎi?*

When used in a **can?** question, the sentence always ends with *dâi?*

Where will you go?
khun jà bpai **thêe-nǎi**?
คุณจะไปที่ไหน

Where is Peter?
Peter yùu **thêe-nǎi**?
ปีเตอร์อยู่ที่ไหน

Where is the post office?
bprai-sà-nee yùu thêe-nǎi?
ไปรษณีย์อยู่ที่ไหน

Where will we eat?
phûuak-rao jà gin thêe-nǎi?
พวกเราจะกินที่ไหน

Where do you want to sit?
khun dtâwng-gaan nâng thêe-nǎi?
คุณต้องการนั่งที่ไหน

Where can we go to swim?
rao bpai wâai-nám thêe-nǎi dâi?
เราไปว่ายน้ำที่ไหนได้

Where is she?
ther yùu thêe-nǎi?
เธออยู่ที่ไหน

Where is my phone?
meuu-thěuu khǎwng-phǒm yùu thêe-nǎi?
มือถือของผมอยู่ที่ไหน

Where can we go?
rao bpai thêe-nǎi dâi?
เราไปที่ไหนได้

Where is he?
khǎo yùu thêe-nǎi?
เขาอยู่ที่ไหน

He is at the bank.
khǎo yùu thêe thá-naa-khaan
เขาอยู่ที่ธนาคาร

Where are we?
phûuak-rao yùu thêe-nǎi?
พวกเราอยู่ที่ไหน

We are at Central.
rao yùu thêe sen-thrân
เราอยู่ที่เซ็นทรัล

Where is she?
ther yùu thêe-nǎi?
เธออยู่ที่ไหน

She is at the bar with Peter.
ther yùu thêe baa gàp Peter
เธออยู่ที่บาร์กับปีเตอร์

Where did you buy your handbag?
khun séuu grà-bpǎo khǎwng-khun thêe-nǎi?
คุณซื้อกระเป๋าของคุณที่ไหน

I bought it **at** Jungceylon.
chǎn séuu **thêe** jang-see-lawn
ฉันซื้อที่จังซีลอน

Note the use of the preposition *thêe* to say something/somebody is 'at' somewhere.

asking and answering 'where?' exercise 18

chapter 8 quiz

Chapter 9

Verb-to-be 3

am, is, are
kheuu
คือ

kheuu is the last of three words used for is, am, are. To avoid confusion, we'll use this one exclusively with people.

That is Mr Peter.
nân kheuu khun Peter
นั่นคือคุณปีเตอร์

She is Ms Jane.
ther kheuu khun Jane
เธอคือคุณเจน

This is Mary.
nêe kheuu Mary
นี่คือแมรี่

He is John.
khăo kheuu John
เขาคือจอห์น

verb-to-be 3

Negative forms

The negative form of the verb-to-be (is, am, are) is the same for *bpen* and *kheuu*, but slightly different for *yùu thêe* and *adjectives*. Let's look at the difference between these:

kheuu

positive form	**negative form**
That **is** John. nân **kheuu** John นั่นคือจอห์น	That is **not** John. nân **mâi châi** John นั่นไม่ใช่จอห์น
He is Peter. khăo kheuu Peter เขาคือปีเตอร์	He is not Peter. khăo mâi châi Peter เขาไม่ใช่ปีเตอร์
This is Jane. nêe kheuu Jane นี่คือเจน	This is not Jane. nêe mâi châi Jane นี่ไม่ใช่เจน

She is Mary.
ther kheuu Mary
เธอคือแมรี่

She is not mary.
ther mâi châi Mary
เธอไม่ใช่แมรี่

bpen

positive form

That **is** a table.
nân **bpen** dtóe
นั่นเป็นโต๊ะ

This is mine.
nêe bpen khăwng-phŏm
นี่เป็นของผม

That is yours.
nân bpen khăwng-khun
นั่นเป็นของคุณ

This is a glass.
nêe bpen gâaeo
นี่เป็นแก้ว

negative form

That **is not** a table.
nân **mâi châi** dtóe
นั่นไม่ใช่โต๊ะ

This is not mine.
nêe mâi châi khăwng-phŏm
นี่ไม่ใช่ของผม

That is not yours.
nân mâi châi khăwng-khun
นั่นไม่ใช่ของคุณ

This is not a glass.
nêe mâi châi gâaeo
นี่ไม่ใช่แก้ว

yùu

positive form

He **is** here.
khăo **yùu** thêe-nêe
เขาอยู่ที่นี่

They are there.
phûuak-khăo yùu thêe-nân
พวกเขาอยู่ที่นั่น

We are at the bar.
rao yùu thêe baa
เราอยู่ที่บาร์

She is at home.
ther yùu thêe bâan
เธออยู่ที่บ้าน

negative form

He **is not** here.
khăo **mâi yùu** thêe-nêe
เขาไม่อยู่ที่นี่

They are not there.
phûuak-khăo mâi yùu thêe-nân
พวกเขาไม่อยู่ที่นั่น

We are not at the bar.
rao mâi yùu thêe baa
เราไม่อยู่ที่บาร์

She is not at home.
ther mâi yùu thêe bâan
เธอไม่อยู่ที่บ้าน

adjectives

positive form	**negative form**
It **is** tall. man sǔung มันสูง	It **is not** tall. man **mâi** sǔung มันไม่สูง
A hot plate. jaan ráwn จานร้อน	The plate is not hot. jaan mâi ráwn จานไม่ร้อน
A long table. dtóe yaao โต๊ะยาว	The table is not long. dtóe mâi yaao โต๊ะไม่ยาว
A heavy handbag. grà-bpǎo nàk กระเป๋าหนัก	The handbag is not heavy. grà-bpǎo mâi nàk กระเป๋าไม่หนัก

exception for colours

positive form	**negative form**
It **is** red. man sěe-daaeng มันสีแดง	It **is not** red. man **mâi châi** sěe-daaeng มันไม่ใช่สีแดง
A black car. ród-yon sěe-dam รถยนต์สีดำ	The car is not black. ród-yon mâi châi sěe-dam รถยนต์ไม่ใช่สีดำ

negative forms

exercise 19

Question tags

You can now construct both positive and negative statements with all three verbs-to-be and with adjectives. These can be made into questions simply by adding a question tag to the end.

The question tag *châi mǎi?* is added to form a question with the verb-to-be or adjectives. It's the same for all statements, irrespective of which verb-to-be, or adjective, or positive or negative. So they're nice and easy to remember!

... isn't it? ... châi măi? ... ใช่ไหม	... aren't I? ... châi măi? ... ใช่ไหม
... isn’t he/she? ... châi măi? ... ใช่ไหม	... aren’t we/they? ... châi măi? ... ใช่ไหม

Answering

Answering is as easy as asking - almost! You can just use *châi* for yes or *mâi châi* for no, **but** it can get a bit confusing if the question tag was on the end of a negative statement.

In the case of negative statements, the answer would mean *yes, it is not*, which is contrary to what you expect from European languages.

question:	He is **not** here, **is he**? khăo **mâi** yùu thêe-nêe, **châi măi**? เขาไม่อยู่ที่นี่ใช่ไหม
answer:	**Yes**, (you are correct) he **is not** here. **châi**, khăo **mâi yùu** thêe-nêe ใช่ เขาไม่อยู่ที่นี่
answer:	**No**, (you are wrong) he **is** here. **mâi châi**, khăo **yùu** thêe-nêe ไม่ใช่ เขาอยู่ที่นี่

Think of it like this: you are making a statement and the question tag is asking for confirmation. So if your statement said something is not, then the answer must be *yes, it is not*, or *no, it is*.

question	**yes**	**no**
That is John, isn't it? nân kheuu John, châi măi? นั่นคือจอห์นใช่ไหม	yes, it is châi ใช่	no, it isn't mâi châi ไม่ใช่

That is a table, isn't it?	yes, it is	no, it isn't
nân bpen dtóe, châi măi?	châi	mâi châi
นั่นเป็นโต๊ะใช่ไหม	ใช่	ไม่ใช่
He is not here, is he?	yes, he's not	no, he is
khăo mâi yùu thêe-nêe, châi măi?	châi	mâi châi
เขาไม่อยู่ที่นี่ใช่ไหม	ใช่	ไม่ใช่
It's not tall, is it?	yes, it's not	no, it is
man mâi sŭung, châi măi?	châi	mâi châi
มันไม่สูงใช่ไหม	ใช่	ไม่ใช่

question tags & answers

chapter 9 quiz

Chapter 10

Classifiers

Put simply: using one thing to count another.

Think of classifiers as similar to the method used when counting uncountable nouns in English; two **loaves of** bread, a **bottle of** beer, a **cup of** coffee. Powders, grains and fluids are typically counted by the containers or measure they come in; a **packet of** tea, a **litre of** water, a **can of** beans, a **kilo of** flour, etc.

In exactly the same way, *everything* in Thai is counted using a classifier.

It's important to use the correct classifier when counting or quantifying more than one object (noun). Each noun has a specific classifier which should be used in the sentence when you are referring to a number of items.

A classifier is generally used with a category of nouns which have a common characteristic, although these groups often seem arbitrary. It's therefore a good idea to memorise the classifier along with the noun when you learn new vocabulary.

New vocabulary

classifiers

person, people
khon
คน

road vehicles (bicycle, motorcycle, car, van, truck, bus)
khan
คัน

a piece from something whole (e.g. pizza, cake, cloth)
chín
ชิ้น

animals, tables, chairs, shirts, trousers, items with limbs
dtuua
ตัว

leaf, sheet, cup, plate, ticket, hat, bag, (sheets & containers)
bai
ใบ

fruit, all kinds of balls, meatballs, most sphere-like objects
lûuk
ลูก

only book and knife
lâem
เล่ม

house, building
lăng
หลัง

room
hâwng
ห้อง

any small item
an
อัน

newspaper, contract, letter, all documents
chà-bàp
ฉบับ

any kind of machinery, including electronics
khrêuuang
เครื่อง

occasions, number of times
khráng
ครั้ง

common classifiers

nouns

friend
phêuuan
เพื่อน

person
khon
คน

bottle
khùuad
ขวด

book năng-sĕuu หนังสือ	ticket dtŭua ตั๋ว	room hâwng ห้อง
document àek-gà-săan เอกสาร	newspaper năng-sĕuu-phim หนังสือพิมพ์	dog măa หมา
cat maaeo แมว	paper grà-dàad กระดาษ	contract săn-yaa สัญญา
house bâan บ้าน	letter jòd-măai จดหมาย	man phûu-chaai ผู้ชาย
woman phûu-yĭng ผู้หญิง	apple áaep-bpêrn แอปเปิ้ล	orange sôm ส้ม

nouns 2

Using classifiers

The sentence form is object + quantity + classifier, like this:

	object	**quantity**	**classifier**
1 table	dtóe โต๊ะ	nèung หนึ่ง	dtuua ตัว
2 chairs	gâo-êe เก้าอี้	săwng สอง	dtuua ตัว
3 knives	mêed มีด	săam สาม	lâem เล่ม
12 apples	áaep-bpêrn แอปเปิ้ล	sìp-săwng สิบสอง	lûuk ลูก
8 cars	ród-yon รถยนต์	bpàaed แปด	khan คัน
6 men	phûu-chaai ผู้ชาย	hòk หก	khon คน

2 TV's	thee-wee ทีวี	sǎwng สอง	khrêuuang เครื่อง

When the object and the classifier are the same, we can leave out the object.

	object	**quantity**	**classifier**
3 people	-	sǎam สาม	khon คน
4 rooms	-	sèe สี่	hâwng ห้อง

There are hundreds of classifiers in Thai, but the small selection here is enough to get you started in everyday conversation. Always use *an* if you are in any doubt - it may be incorrrect, but you'll be understood.

There's a list of the most common classifiers in appendix I.

using classifiers

exercise 20

chapter 10 quiz

Psst! There's some bonus material after the online exercise.

Chapter 11

Have

have, has
mee
มี

We use the verb *mee* to say that someone/something possesses or has something. It goes before the item in the sentence, for example:

I **have** a house.
chăn **mee** bâan
ฉันมีบ้าน

She **has** two dogs.
ther **mee** măa săwng dtuua
เธอมีหมาสองตัว

We **have** a ticket.
phûuak-rao **mee** dtŭua
พวกเรามีตั๋ว

He **has** three books.
khăo **mee** năng-sĕuu săam lâem
เขามีหนังสือสามเล่ม

It is not necessary to use the classifier to say you have only one of something. Look at the difference between singular and plural.

plural

singular

subject	mee	object	quantity	classifier
I	have	**a house**.		
chăn	mee	bâan		
ฉัน	มี	บ้าน		
I	have	**three houses**.		
chăn	mee	bâan	săam	lăng
ฉัน	มี	บ้าน	สาม	หลัง

She	has	a dog.		
ther	mee	măa		
เธอ	มี	หมา		
She	has	two dogs.		
ther	mee	măa	săwng	dtuua
เธอ	มี	หมา	สอง	ตัว
He	has	a friend.		
khăo	mee	phêuuan		
เขา	มี	เพื่อน		
He	has	seven friends.		
khăo	mee	phêuuan	jèd	khon
เขา	มี	เพื่อน	เจ็ด	คน
They	have	a car.		
phûuak-khăo	mee	ród-yon		
พวกเขา	มี	รถยนต์		
They	have	two cars.		
phûuak-khăo	mee	ród-yon	săwng	khan
พวกเขา	มี	รถยนต์	สอง	คัน

have, has

exercise 21

Not have

To say that we *do not have* something we simply place the negative word *mâi* in front of *mee*. It is the same format as singular above, in that we don't need a classifier.

I **don’t have** a house.
chăn **mâi mee** bâan
ฉันไม่มีบ้าน

He **doesn’t have** any friends.
khăo **mâi mee** phêuuan
เขาไม่มีเพื่อน

She doesn’t have any jeans.
ther mâi mee gaang-gaeng-yeen
เธอไม่มีกางเกงยีนส์

This hotel doesn't have a restaurant.
roong-raaem née mâi mee ráan-aa-hăan
โรงแรมนี้ไม่มีร้านอาหาร

This bar doesn't have Chang beer.
baa née mâi mee biia Chang
บาร์นี้ไม่มีเบียร์ช้าง

not have exercise 22

Do you have?

We can ask questions using *mee* with the question word *măi*?:

Do you **have** a house?
khun **mee** bâan **măi**?
คุณมีบ้านไหม

Does Peter **have** any friends?
Peter **mee** phêuuan **măi**?
ปีเตอร์มีเพื่อนไหม

Does this shop have any coffee?
ráan née mee gaa-faae măi?
ร้านนี้มีกาแฟไหม

Note the different pronunciation to *nêe* and *nân*, which are pronouns (page 43). These words are modifiers and are both high tone.

Does Jane have a phone?
Jane mee meuu-thĕuu măi?
เจนมีมือถือไหม

Do we have any pizza?
rao mee phíd-sâa măi?
เรามีพิซซ่าไหม

There is & There are

We also use *mee* to say 'there is ...' and 'there are ...'.

There is a car here.
mee ród thêe-nêe
มีรถที่นี่

There are jeans and a T-shirt.
mee gaang-gaeng-yeen láe sêuua-yêuud
มีกางเกงยีนส์และเสื้อยืด

Do they have pizza here? (Is pizza available here?)
thêe-nêe mee phíd-sâa măi?
ที่นี่มีพิซซ่าไหม

do you have? exercise 23

Want to have/to get

We are already familiar with *yàak* to say we want to do something. If we combine it with *dâi*, the meaning changes. Here are two ways to say we want to have/to get something.

want to have/to get	want to have/to get
ao	yàak dâi
เอา	อยากได้

As these words are to say we *want* something, they are always used with a noun. Let's look at *ao* first. Questions are answered yes/no using *ao* and *mâi ao*, or *yàak dâi* and *mâi yàak dâi*.

Do you **want** coffee?
ao gaa-faae măi?
เอากาแฟไหม

Yes please.
ao khráp
เอาครับ

No thanks.
mâi ao khráp
ไม่เอาครับ

Does he **want** this book?
khăo **ao** năng-sĕuu lâem née măi?
เขาเอาหนังสือเล่มนี้ไหม

Yes, he does.
khăo **ao**
เขาเอา

No, he doesn't.
khăo **mâi ao**
เขาไม่เอา

It is exactly the same with *yàak dâi*. We'll use the same examples.

Do you **want** coffee?
yàak dâi gaa-faae măi?
อยากได้กาแฟไหม

Yes please.
yàak dâi khráp
อยากได้ครับ

No thanks.
mâi yàak dâi khráp
ไม่อยากได้ครับ

Does he **want** this book?
khăo **yàak dâi** năng-sěuu lâem née măi?
เขาอยากได้หนังสือเล่มนี้ไหม

Yes, he does.
khăo **yàak dâi**
เขาอยากได้

No, he doesn't.
khăo **mâi yàak dâi**
เขาไม่อยากได้

Summary of 'want to'

dtâwng-gaan & yàak (jà)

Used with verbs to say we want to *do* something.

ao & yàak dâi

Used with nouns to say we want to *have* something.

want to have

chapter 11 quiz

Chapter 12

Quantifiers

So what exactly are quantifiers?

A quantifier is a word that *usually* goes after a noun to express an uncertain quantity of an object; for example 'a **little** coffee' or '**a lot** of bread'.

There are many quantifiers in Thai and they can be confusing at first. In this chapter we'll introduce some quantifiers and provide examples for each one.

There are quantifiers to describe large quantities (a lot, much), small quantities (a little, a bit, a few) and undefined quantities (some).

Some quantifiers are used with countable nouns and others are used with uncountable nouns. The first quantifiers we'll cover in this chapter are used to talk about a quantity of something *countable*, instead of an exact number of something. However, we still use these with the classifier, just as if we were using a number.

many, a lot lăai หลาย	not many, a few mâi gèe ไม่กี่

These use the same sentence form as a numbered quantity with a classifier from chapter 10.

subject	**mee**	**object**	**quantity**	**classifier**
She	has	a dog.		
ther	mee	măa		
เธอ	มี	หมา		
She	has	two dogs.		
ther	mee	măa	săwng	dtuua
เธอ	มี	หมา	สอง	ตัว
She	has	many dogs.		
ther	mee	măa	**lăai**	dtuua
เธอ	มี	หมา	หลาย	ตัว

She doesn't	have	many dogs.		
ther	mee	mǎa	**mâi gèe**	dtuua
เธอ	มี	หมา	ไม่กี่	ตัว

Of course, the classifier is still left out if it's the same as the object.

many

many people
lǎai khon
หลายคน

many cars
ród-yon **lǎai** khan
รถยนต์หลายคัน

many books
nǎng-sěuu lǎai lâem
หนังสือหลายเล่ม

many houses
bâan lǎai lǎng
บ้านหลายหลัง

many rooms
lǎai hâwng
หลายห้อง

many newspapers
nǎng-sěuu-phim lǎai chà-bàp
หนังสือพิมพ์หลายฉบับ

Examples as sentences:

Peter has **many** friends.
Peter mee phêuuan **lǎai** khon
ปีเตอร์มีเพื่อนหลายคน

Jane drank many cups of coffee.
Jane dèuum gaa-faae lǎai thûuai
เจนดื่มกาแฟหลายถ้วย

He has many pairs of shorts.
khǎo mee gaang-gaeng-khǎa-sân lǎai dtuua
เขามีกางเกงขาสั้นหลายตัว

She ate many slices of pizza.
ther gin phíd-sâa lǎai chín
เธอกินพิซซ่าหลายชิ้น

We made many contracts with him.
rao tham sǎn-yaa lǎai chà-bàp gàp khǎo
เราทำสัญญาหลายฉบับกับเขา

How much did you buy that house for?
khun séuu bâan lǎng nán raa-khaa thâo-rài?
คุณซื้อบ้านหลังนั้นราคาเท่าไหร่

Many millions of Baht.
lăai láan bàad
หลายล้านบาท

Jane read many books.
Jane àan năng-sĕuu lăai lâem
เจนอ่านหนังสือหลายเล่ม

My house has many rooms.
bâan khăwng-phŏm mee lăai hâwng
บ้านของผมมีหลายห้อง

many — exercise 24

not many

The form is the same for *mâi gèe*.

a **few** people
mâi gèe khon
ไม่กี่คน

a few books
năng-sĕuu mâi gèe lâem
หนังสือไม่กี่เล่ม

not many rooms
mâi gèe hâwng
ไม่กี่ห้อง

not many cars
ród-yon **mâi gèe** khan
รถยนต์ไม่กี่คัน

not many houses
bâan mâi gèe lăng
บ้านไม่กี่หลัง

a few newspapers
năng-sĕuu-phim mâi gèe chà-bàp
หนังสือพิมพ์ไม่กี่ฉบับ

And using the same sentence examples:

Peter **doesn't** have **many** friends.
Peter mee phêuuan **mâi gèe** khon
ปีเตอร์มีเพื่อนไม่กี่คน

Jane didn't drink many cups of coffee.
Jane dèuum gaa-faae mâi gèe thûuai
เจนดื่มกาแฟไม่กี่ถ้วย

He doesn't have many pairs of shorts.
khăo mee gaang-gaeng-khăa-sân mâi gèe dtuua
เขามีกางเกงขาสั้นไม่กี่ตัว

She didn't eat many slices of pizza.
ther gin phíd-sâa mâi gèe chín
เธอกินพิซซ่าไม่กี่ชิ้น

We made a few contracts with him.
rao tham săn-yaa mâi gèe chà-bàp gàp khăo
เราทำสัญญาไม่กี่ฉบับกับเขา

How much did you buy that house for?
khun séuu bâan lăng nán raa-khaa thâo-rài?
คุณซื้อบ้านหลังนั้นราคาเท่าไหร่

A few million Baht.
mâi gèe láan bàad
ไม่กี่ล้านบาท

Jane hasn't read many books.
Jane àan năng-sĕuu mâi gèe lâem
เจนอ่านหนังสือไม่กี่เล่ม

My house doesn't have many rooms.
bâan khăwng-phŏm mee mâi gèe hâwng
บ้านของผมมีไม่กี่ห้อง

not many

exercise 25

solitary

---

only one, just one, alone
diaao
เดียว

The sentence format changes a little, object + classifier + *diaao*. Again, we drop the classifier if it's the same as the object.

only one man
phûu-chaai khon **diaao**
ผู้ชายคนเดียว

only one dog
măa dtuua diaao
หมาตัวเดียว

just one person
khon **diaao**
คนเดียว

just one room
hâwng diaao
ห้องเดียว

only one book
nǎng-sěuu lâem diaao
หนังสือเล่มเดียว

just one apple
áaep-bpêrn lûuk diaao
แอปเปิ้ลลูกเดียว

only one TV
thee-wee khrêuuang diaao
ทีวีเครื่องเดียว

just one time (just once)
khráng diaao
ครั้งเดียว

We also use *diaao* to mean 'alone', at the end of the sentence following the classifier.

I am sitting here **alone**.
chǎn nâng thêe-nêe **khon diaao**
ฉันนั่งที่นี่คนเดียว

Jane came alone.
Jane maa khon diaao
เจนมาคนเดียว

Peter will drive to Bangkok alone.
Peter jà khàp ród bpai grung-thâep khon diaao
ปีเตอร์จะขับรถไปกรุงเทพคนเดียว

only one

exercise 26

Measures

When we measure a quantity of a material, the weights and measures we use are also classifiers. Here are some common weight and liquid measures.

100 grams
khèed
ขีด

litre
líd
ลิตร

kilogram
gì-loo
กิโล

half
khrêung
ครึ่ง

Some essentials for the shopping basket.

rice
khâao
ข้าว

tea
chaa
ชา

sugar
nám-dtaan
น้ำตาล

milk
nom
นม

apple juice
nám-áaep-bpêrn
น้ำแอปเปิ้ล

chicken
gài
ไก่

orange juice
nám-sôm
น้ำส้ม

pork
mŭu
หมู

cooking oil
nám-man-phêuud
น้ำมันพืช

beef
néuua
เนื้อ

The measure acts as the classifier, like this:

5 **kilos** of rice
khâao hâa **gì-loo**
ข้าว 5 กิโล

200 grams of tea
chaa **săwng khèed**
ชา 2 ขีด

half a kilo of sugar
nám-dtaan khrêung gì-loo
น้ำตาลครึ่งกิโล

a litre of milk
nom nèung líd
นมหนึ่งลิตร

150 grams of chicken
gài nèung khèed khrêung
ไก่ 1 ขีดครึ่ง

3 bottles of cooking oil
nám-man-phêuud săam khùuad
น้ำมันพืช 3 ขวด

half a kilo of beef
néuua khrêung gì-loo
เนื้อครึ่งกิโล

Example sentences:

I drank **four bottles** of beer.
phŏm dèuum biia **sèe khùuad**
ผมดื่มเบียร์สี่ขวด

She bought 2 kilos of sugar.
ther séuu nám-dtaan săwng gì-loo
เธอซื้อน้ำตาล 2 กิโล

We ate 1½ kilos of beef.
rao gin néuua nèung gì-loo khrêung
เรากินเนื้อ 1 กิโลครึ่ง

measures exercise 27

How many?

how many?
gèe?
กี่

The word *gèe* which we used in 'not many' (*mâi gèe*) is also used to ask 'how many' by changing its position in the sentence. Questions concerning quantity must be asked using the correct classifier. Sentence format is like this:

how many ... *object* ... do you have?
khun mee ... *object* ... gèe ... *classifier* ...?
คุณมี ... กี่ ...

Example sentences:

How many cars do you have?
khun mee ród-yon **gèe** khan?
คุณมีรถยนต์กี่คัน

How many rooms does this house have?
bâan lăng née mee gèe hâwng?
บ้านหลังนี้มีกี่ห้อง

How many friends does he have?
khăo mee phêuuan gèe khon?
เขามีเพื่อนกี่คน

How many tickets will you buy?
khun jà séuu dtŭua gèe bai?
คุณจะซื้อตั๋วกี่ใบ

How many bottles of beer did he drink?
khăo dèuum biia gèe khùuad?
เขาดื่มเบียร์กี่ขวด

How many houses does this village have?
mùu-bâan née mee bâan gèe lăng?
หมู่บ้านนี้มีบ้านกี่หลัง

How many plates of rice do you want?
khun dtâwng-gaan khâao gèe jaan?
คุณต้องการข้าวกี่จาน

how many

exercise 28

chapter 12 quiz

Chapter 13

Time indicators

We can add a day of the week to our sentences to indicate when a future event will take place. Almost always the time indicator will come at the end, but it is possible to put it at the front as in the second example below. Remember that *mâi-dâi* always comes at the end of a sentence.

I will go there **on Monday**.
chăn jà bpai thêe-nân **wan-jan**
ฉันจะไปที่นั่นวันจันทร์

On Monday I will go to Bangkok.
wan-jan chăn jà bpai grung-thâep
วันจันทร์ฉันจะไปกรุงเทพ

Will she come on Tuesday?
ther jà maa wan-ang-khaan măi?
เธอจะมาวันอังคารไหม

I will speak with you on Thursday.
phŏm jà phûud gàp khun wan-phá-réu-hàd
ผมจะพูดกับคุณวันพฤหัส

He will buy a car on Saturday.
khăo jà séuu ród-yon wan-săo
เขาจะซื้อรถยนต์วันเสาร์

They cannot come on Sunday.
phûuak-khăo maa wan-aa-thíd mâi-dâi
พวกเขามาวันอาทิตย์ไม่ได้

using days of the week — exercise 29

Points in time

day	week	month
wan	aa-thíd	deuuan
วัน	อาทิตย์	เดือน

year
bpee
ปี

now
dtawn-née
ตอนนี้

today
wan-née
วันนี้

tomorrow
phrûng-née
พรุ่งนี้

yesterday
mêuua-waan-née
เมื่อวานนี้

this month
deuuan-née
เดือนนี้

next month
deuuan-nâa
เดือนหน้า

last month
deuuan-thêe-láeo
เดือนที่แล้ว

this year
bpee-née
ปีนี้

next year
bpee-nâa
ปีหน้า

last year
bpee-thêe-láeo
ปีที่แล้ว

the day after tomorrow
wan-má-reuun-née
วันมะรืนนี้

the day before yesterday
mêuua-waan-seuun
เมื่อวานซืน

points in time

exercise 30

Modifiers

next
nâa
หน้า

last, ago, previous
thêe-láeo
ที่แล้ว

in, more
èek
อีก

within
phaai-nai
ภายใน

As with days of the week, we can add a point in time at the end of a statement or question, or combine them with a modifying word. Note that *èek* normally comes at the beginning.

He will come **today**.
khăo jà maa **wan-née**
เขาจะมาวันนี้

I want to eat now.
chăn dtâwng-gaan gin dtawn-née
ฉันต้องการกินตอนนี้

We will go swimming this week.
phûuak-rao jà bpai wâai-nám aa-thíd-née
พวกเราจะไปว่ายน้ำอาทิตย์นี้

They came the day before yesterday.
phûuak-khăo maa mêuua-waan-seuun
พวกเขามาเมื่อวานซืน

We will go to Bangkok next week.
rao jà bpai grung-thâep aa-thíd-nâa
เราจะไปกรุงเทพอาทิตย์หน้า

They came to Phuket last year.
phûuak-khăo maa phuu-gèd bpee-thêe-láeo
พวกเขามาภูเก็ตปีที่แล้ว

We will know within four days.
rao jà rúu phaai-nai sèe wan
เราจะรู้ภายในสี่วัน

In three days he will go to Hadyai.
èek săam wan khăo jà bpai hàad-yài
อีกสามวันเขาจะไปหาดใหญ่

modifiers

exercise 31

Parts of the day

morning
dtawn-cháo
ตอนเช้า

midday
glaang-wan
กลางวัน

evening
dtawn-khâm
ตอนค่ำ

afternoon (1pm - 5pm)
dtawn-bàai
ตอนบ่าย

afternoon (5pm - 6pm)
dtawn-yen
ตอนเย็น

night
dtawn-glaang-kheuun
ตอนกลางคืน

this morning
dtawn-cháo-née
ตอนเช้านี้

this afternoon
dtawn-bàai-née
ตอนบ่ายนี้

this evening
dtawn-khâm-née
ตอนค่ำนี้

tonight
kheuun-née
คืนนี้

Mealtimes

breakfast
aa-hăan-cháo
อาหารเช้า

lunch
aa-hăan glaang-wan
อาหารกลางวัน

dinner
aa-hăan-yen
อาหารเย็น

snack
aa-hăan-wâang
อาหารว่าง

to eat, to dine
gin aa-hăan, thaan aa-hăan
กินอาหาร, ทานอาหาร

Sentence examples.

We will go swimming **tomorrow morning**.
rao jà bpai wâai-nám **phrûng-née dtawn-cháo**
เราจะไปว่ายน้ำพรุ่งนี้ตอนเช้า

I will come here next Thursday evening.
chăn jà maa thêe-nêe wan-phá-réu-hàd nâa dtawn-khâm
ฉันจะมาที่นี่วันพฤหัสหน้าตอนค่ำ

We want to eat lunch now.
phûuak-rao dtâwng-gaan gin aa-hăan glaang-wan dtawn-née
พวกเราต้องการกินอาหารกลางวันตอนนี้

Where do you want to eat dinner tomorrow?
khun dtâwng-gaan gin aa-hăan-yen thêe-năi phrûng-née?
คุณต้องการกินอาหารเย็นที่ไหนพรุ่งนี้

We have a snack at lunchtime.
rao gin aa-hăan-wâang dtawn-bàai
เรากินอาหารว่างตอนบ่าย

Would you like to have breakfast with Peter next Thursday?
khun yàak-jà gin aa-hăan-cháo gàp Peter wan-phá-réu-hàd nâa măi?
คุณอยากจะกินอาหารเช้ากับปีเตอร์วันพฤหัสหน้าไหม

parts of the day & mealtimes

exercise 32

chapter 13 quiz

Chapter 14

Question words

As with most question words, these all usually come at the very end of a sentence.

Remember that Thai uses tones, so you need to be careful with your pronunciation when using question words. In English, we often raise our pitch at the end of a question, but this should be avoided in Thai as it messes up the tones of the words you are trying to say.

when?

when?
mêuua-rài?
เมื่อไหร่

When will you go to Bangkok?
khun jà bpai grung-thâep **mêuua-rài**?
คุณจะไปกรุงเทพเมื่อไหร่

When did she come?
ther maa mêuua-rài?
เธอมาเมื่อไหร่

When will we go to swim?
phûuak-rao jà bpai wâai-nám mêuua-rài?
พวกเราจะไปว่ายน้ำเมื่อไหร่

what?

what?
à-rai?
อะไร

What are you doing?
khun tham **à-rai**?
คุณทำอะไร

What did you say?
khun phûud à-rai?
คุณพูดอะไร

What is she doing here?
ther tham à-rai thêe-nêe?
เธอทำอะไรที่นี่

why?

why?
tham-mai?
ทำไม

Why are you sitting here?
khun nâng thêe-nêe **tham-mai**?
คุณนั่งที่นี่ทำไม

Why did she come yesterday?
ther maa mêuua-waan-née tham-mai?
เธอมาเมื่อวานนี้ทำไม

Why did you go there?
tham-mai khun bpai thêe-nân?
ทำไมคุณไปที่นั่น

how?

how?
yàang-rai?
อย่างไร

How will you go to Bangkok?
khun jà bpai grung-thâep **yàang-rai**?
คุณจะไปกรุงเทพอย่างไร

How can you eat that?
khun gin nân dâi yàang-rai?
คุณกินนั่นได้อย่างไร

How can you remember?
khun jam dâi yàang-rai?
คุณจำได้อย่างไร

questions words exercise 33

Chapter 15

More conjunctions

that

---

that, as
wâa
ว่า

The conjunction *wâa* most often follows a verb of speech, thought or something to do with the mind. We already know some verbs we can use *wâa* with right away.

Up to this point we've been careful to only work with vocabulary that had previously been introduced in the book. From hereon, you may come across new words in the example sentences, but it will only be the occasional useful vocabulary and will have an explanation with it.

The form is subject + verb + *wâa* + context

subject	verb	*wâa*	context
He	said	that	he will not wait for us.
khăo	phûud	wâa	khăo jà mâi raw rao
เขา	พูด	ว่า	เขาจะไม่รอเรา

She **said that** she would like to be able to understand Thai.
ther **phûud wâa** ther yàak khâo-jai phaa-săa thai dâi
เธอพูดว่าเธออยากเข้าใจภาษาไทยได้

He knows that you'll like it.
khăo rúu wâa khun jà châwp
เขารู้ว่าคุณจะชอบ

They know that I don't want to go with them.
phûuak-khăo rúu wâa chăn mâi yàak bpai gàp phûuak-khăo
พวกเขารู้ว่าฉันไม่อยากไปกับพวกเขา

I think that it will rain this afternoon.
phŏm khíd wâa fŏn jà dtòk dtawn-bàai-née
ผมคิดว่าฝนจะตกตอนบ่ายนี้
(rain = fŏn, fall = dtòk, rain will fall = fŏn jà dtòk)

She thinks that I don't know.
ther khíd wâa phŏm mâi rúu
เธอคิดว่าผมไม่รู้

He doesn't understand why I don't like to drink beer.
khăo mâi khâo-jai wâa tham-mai phŏm mâi châwp dèuum biia
เขาไม่เข้าใจว่าทำไมผมไม่ชอบดื่มเบียร์

They understand that we'll buy a house next month.
phûuak-khăo khâo-jai wâa rao jà séuu bâan deuuan-nâa
พวกเขาเข้าใจว่าเราจะซื้อบ้านเดือนหน้า

The next two examples use the verb *dâi*, so take note of the slightly different construction for 'can' and 'cannot' (coming between the verb and *wâa*).

I **don't remember that** he wanted to go alone.
chăn **jam mâi-dâi wâa** khăo yàak bpai khon diaao
ฉันจำไม่ได้ว่าเขาอยากไปคนเดียว

I (can) **remember that** I **said that** I wouldn't eat here again.
phŏm **jam dâi wâa** phŏm **phûud wâa** phŏm jà mâi gin thêe-nêe èek
ผมจำได้ว่าผมพูดว่าผมจะไม่กินที่นี่อีก

I heard that you are going to Bangkok tomorrow.
chăn dâi-yin wâa khun jà bpai grung-thâep phrûng-née
ฉันได้ยินว่าคุณจะไปกรุงเทพพรุ่งนี้

I don't see how she could know.
chăn mâi hĕn wâa ther jà rúu dâi yàang-rai
ฉันไม่เห็นว่าเธอจะรู้ได้อย่างไร

I forgot that she doesn't like to walk to work.
phŏm leuum wâa ther mâi châwp dern bpai tham-ngaan
ผมลืมว่าเธอไม่ชอบเดินไปทำงาน

He forgot that we are going to the bank today.
khăo leuum wâa phûuak-rao jà bpai thá-naa-khaan wan-née
เขาลืมว่าพวกเราจะไปธนาคารวันนี้

That reads as 'No Entry'.
nân àan wâa 'hâam khâo'
นั่นอ่านว่า 'ห้ามเข้า'

She wrote that she doesn't love me.
ther khĭian wâa ther mâi rák phŏm
เธอเขียนว่าเธอไม่รักผม

There are two new words worth introducing here, which can be used almost interchangeably with two verbs we already know.

say, tell (similar usage to *speak*) bàwk บอก	suppose (similar usage to *think*) néuk นึก

He **said that** he can't come.
khăo **bàwk wâa** khăo maa mâi-dâi
เขาบอกว่าเขามาไม่ได้

She said that she would like to go to the new restaurant.
ther bàwk wâa ther yàak bpai ráan-aa-hăan mài
เธอบอกว่าเธออยากไปร้านอาหารใหม่

I told him that I was very busy.
phŏm bàwk khăo wâa phŏm yûng mâak
ผมบอกเขาว่าผมยุ่งมาก

He said he's busy.
khăo wâa khăo yûng
เขาว่าเขายุ่ง

As we've said before, lazy speakers will drop words. You will often here Thai speakers drop the word *bàwk* as in the previous example.

They **thought that** we wouldn't come with them.
phûuak-khăo **néuk wâa** rao jà mâi maa gàp phûuak-khăo
พวกเขานึกว่าเราจะไม่มากับพวกเขา

I thought that there would be no work today.
chăn néuk wâa wan-née jà mâi mee ngaan
ฉันนึกว่าวันนี้จะไม่มีงาน
(the verb 'to work' = tham-ngaan, the noun 'work' = ngaan)

I can't think who he is.
phŏm néuk mâi àwk wâa khăo bpen khrai
ผมนึกไม่ออกว่าเขาเป็นใคร

conjunction 'that'

but

---

but
dtàae
แต่

The conjunction *dtàae* is used when we want to give some extra information that *contrasts* with the previous part of the sentence. You will see in the examples that it's placed between two opposing ideas.

The form is clause 1 + *dtàae* + clause 2

clause 1	***dtàae***	**clause 2**
I can do it	but	I don't want to.
chăn tham dâi	dtàae	chăn mâi yàak tham
ฉันทำได้	แต่	ฉันไม่อยากทำ

I can't go with you, **but** I can go alone.
phŏm bpai gàp khun mâi-dâi, **dtàae** phŏm bpai khon-diaao dâi
ผมไปกับคุณไม่ได้ แต่ผมไปคนเดียวได้

I don't have a house, but I have a car.
phŏm mâi mee bâan, dtàae phŏm mee ród-yon
ผมไม่มีบ้าน แต่ผมมีรถยนต์

This hotel does not have big rooms, but it has a restaurant.
roong-raaem née mâi mee hâwng yài, dtàae man mee ráan-aa-hăan
โรงแรมนี้ไม่มีห้องใหญ่ แต่มันมีร้านอาหาร

You can't sit here, but you can sit there.
khun nâng thêe-nêe mâi-dâi, dtàae khun nâng thêe-nân dâi
คุณนั่งที่นี่ไม่ได้ แต่คุณนั่งที่นั่นได้

I can't speak English, but I can speak Thai.
chăn phûud phaa-săa ang-grìd mâi-dâi, dtàae chăn phûud phaa-săa thai dâi
ฉันพูดภาษาอังกฤษไม่ได้ แต่ฉันพูดภาษาไทยได้

I can't walk with you, but I can wait here.
chăn dern gàp khun mâi-dâi, dtàae chăn raw thêe-nêe dâi
ฉันเดินกับคุณไม่ได้ แต่ฉันรอที่นี่ได้

conjunction 'but'

Chapter 16

Telling the time

asking the time

what time is it? waeh-laa thâo-rài? เวลาเท่าไหร่	what time is it? gèe moong láeo? กี่โมงแล้ว

time vocabulary

second wí-naa-thee วินาที	minute naa-thee นาที	hour chûua-moong ชั่วโมง
half khrêung ครึ่ง	exactly dtrong ตรง	o'clock moong โมง
12 noon thîiang-wan เที่ยงวัน	12 midnight thîiang-kheuun เที่ยงคืน	at dtawn ตอน

In everyday conversation, Thai speakers will often shorten the word *wí-naa-thee* to just *wí.*

parts of the day

In chapter 13 we learned the names for parts of the day. We'll use the same words here when telling the time, along with two new ones for early morning and evening.

1am to 5am dtee ตี	morning cháo เช้า	early afternoon bàai บ่าย
late afternoon yen เย็น	evening thûm ทุ่ม	

o'clock

The following clock face shows the time on the hour for the 12-hour period from midnight to 11 a.m.

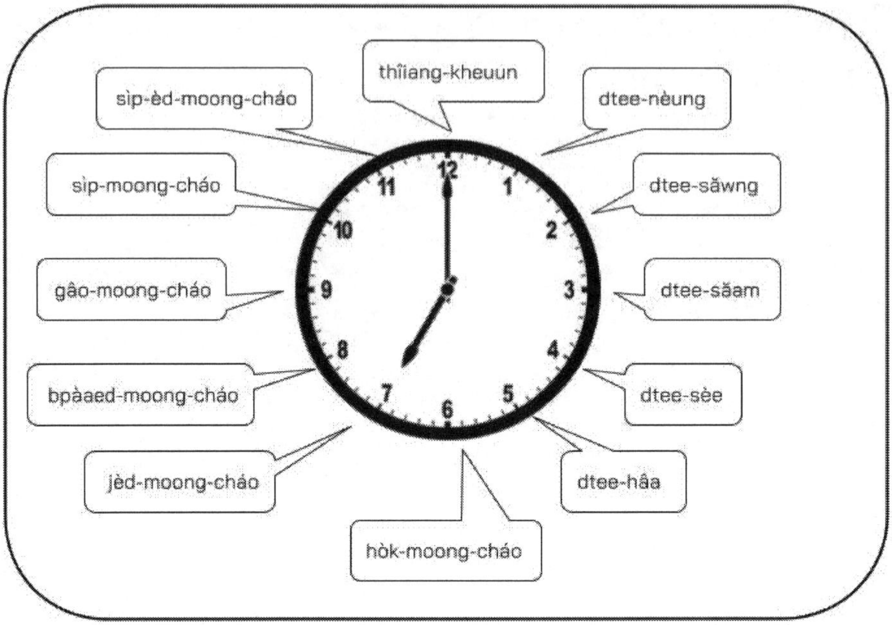

midnight to 5 a.m.

After midnight (*thîiang-kheuun*), between 1 a.m. and 5 a.m. the word for 'o'clock' in this period is *dtee*. We simply put the word *dtee* in front of the number.

I went to bed (at) **2 a.m.**
chǎn bpai nawn (dtawn) **dtee-sǎwng**
ฉันไปนอน(ตอน)ตีสอง
(using *dtawn* is optional - all these sentence are fine without it)

6 a.m. to 11 a.m.

From 6 a.m. until 11 a.m. the word 'o'clock' for this period is *moong* along with the word for morning, *cháo*. We put the number in front of *moong-cháo*.

He opens the shop **6 a.m.**
khǎo bpèrd ráan **hòk-moong-cháo**
เขาเปิดร้านหกโมงเช้า

We drive to work at **8 a.m.**
rao khàp ród bpai tham-ngaan **bpàaed-moong-cháo**
เราขับรถไปทำงานแปดโมงเช้า

If the time is exactly on the hour, we can add *dtrong*:

What time is it?
gèe moong láeo?
กี่โมงแล้ว

It's exactly 9 o'clock.
gâo-moong dtrong
เก้าโมงตรง

The next clock face shows the time on the hour for the 12-hour period from noon (midday) to 11 p.m.

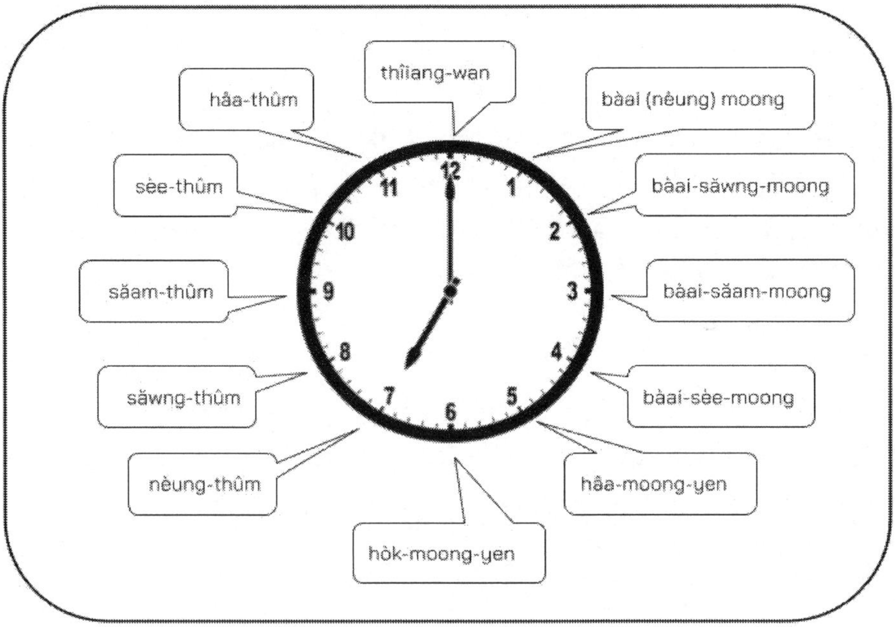

noon to 4 p.m.

After midday (*thîiang-wan*), between 1 p.m. and 4 p.m. we use the word for early afternoon, *bàai*, followed by the number, then the word 'o'clock' for this period, which is *moong* again.

I have lunch at **1 p.m.**
chăn gin aa-hăan-glaang-wan dtawn-bàai-**moong**
ฉันกินอาหารกลางวันตอนบ่ายโมง

Note: for 1 p.m. we don't say *nèung-moong*, we say *bàai-moong*.

She will be waiting for us at **3 p.m.**
ther jà raw rao dtawn-bàai-**săam-moong**
เธอจะรอเราตอนบ่ายสามโมง

Note: Thai speakers will often drop the *moong* when there's a number, like this:

ther jà raw rao dtawn-bàai**-săam** ~~moong~~

5 p.m. to 6 p.m.

From 5 p.m. to 6 p.m. the word 'o'clock' for this period is *moong* along with the word for late afternoon, *yen*. We put the number in front of *moong-yen*.

I have dinner at **6 p.m.**
chăn gin aa-hăan-yen dtawn **hòk-moong-yen**
ฉันกินอาหารเย็นตอนหกโมงเย็น

Note: you may sometimes hear *sèe-moong-yen* instead of *bàai-sèe-moong* or *sèe-moong*. Either is acceptable.

7 p.m. to 11 p.m.

Between 7 p.m. and 11 p.m. the word for 'o'clock' in this period is *thûm*. We simply put the word *thûm* after the number.

This period of the day is unusual because we start counting from 1 to 5 again, rather than using 7 to 11.

I go to bed at **10 p.m.**
chăn bpai nawn dtawn **sèe-thûm**
ฉันไปนอนตอนสี่ทุ่ม

parts of the hour

Up to half-past the hour, we say the hour of the day followed by the number of minutes, for example:

3:00 a.m.
dtee-săam
ตีสาม

12:10 a.m.
thîiang-kheuun sìp naa-thee
เที่ยงคืนสิบนาที

4:15 p.m.
bàai-sèe-moong sìp-hâa naa-thee
บ่ายสี่โมงสิบห้านาที

5:05 p.m.
hâa-moong yen **hâa naa-thee**
ห้าโมงเย็นห้านาที

7:10 a.m.
jèd-moong (cháo) sìp naa-thee
เจ็ดโมง(เช้า)สิบนาที

2:20 a.m.
dtee-săwng yêe-sìp naa-thee
ตีสองยี่สิบนาที

9:25 p.m.
săam-thûm yêe-sìp-hâa naa-thee
สามทุ่มยี่สิบห้านาที

6:30 p.m.
hòk-moong khrêung
หกโมงครึ่ง

12:30 p.m.
thîiang khrêung
เที่ยงครึ่ง

In the 6.30 p.m. example, we don't include the word *yen*. Whenever the time is half-past, we just say the hour with half.

From half-past up to the hour can be said in two ways. Either the same as above, counting minutes past the hour, like this:

2:40 a.m.
dtee-săwng **sèe-sìp naa-thee**
ตีสองสี่สิบนาที

6:55 p.m.
hòk-moong (yen) hâa-sìp-hâa naa-thee
หกโมง(เย็น)ห้าสิบห้านาที

12:35 a.m.
thîiang-kheuun săam-sìp-hâa naa-thee
เที่ยงคืนสามสิบห้านาที

8:50 a.m.
bpàaed-moong (cháo) hâa-sìp naa-thee
แปดโมง(เช้า)ห้าสิบนาที

Or, more commonly, by using *èek* to say how many 'more' minutes remain to the hour:

4:35 a.m.
èek yêe-sìp hâa naa-thee dtee-hâa
อีกยี่สิบห้านาทีตีห้า

7:40 p.m.
èek yêe-sìp naa-thee săwng-thûm
อีกยี่สิบนาทีสองทุ่ม

12:45 a.m.
èek sìp-hâa naa-thee dtee-nèung
อีกสิบห้านาทีตีหนึ่ง

3:50 a.m.
èek sìp naa-thee dtee-sèe
อีกสิบนาทีตีสี่

4:55 p.m.
èek hâa naa-thee hâa-moong-yen
อีกห้านาทีห้าโมงเย็น

12:55 p.m.
èek hâa naa-thee bàai moong
อีกห้านาทีบ่ายโมง

telling the time

exercise 34

Section 2

This section introduces all the other elements that make up the language. Each chapter will introduce a concept followed by examples to illustrate usage.

You'll learn how to make comparisons, how to use relative pronouns and some more quantifiers. There are chapters on prepositions of place and time to say where or when something is, and there are words to express need and necessity.

You'll learn how to talk about possibility and use 'if' and 'because'. The adverbs of frequency will show you how to talk about how often something happens, and the chapter on prefixes will expand your vocabulary instantly.

The section closes with ways to talk about the past and who's who in family relations.

Only a small amount of new vocabulary is introduced in this section (some may appear as new words in examples, where they will be explained), and there are no exercises.

It's not necessary to study this section in chapter order - it can be used equally well as a reference.

Chapter 17

Which & that

Which?	that (as a relative pronoun)
năi?	thêe
ไหน	ที่

new vocabulary (all verbs)

study
riian
เรียน

meet
phóp, jer
พบ, เจอ

chat, talk
khui
คุย

use
chái
ใช้

shop
séuu-khăwng
ซื้อของ

Which?

To ask 'which object/person?', we must use the correct classifier in the format:

object + classifier + *năi*?

Which man?
phûu-chaai khon **năi**?
ผู้ชายคนไหน

Which two tables?
dtóe săwng dtuua năi?
โต๊ะสองตัวไหน

Which bookshop?
ráan-khăai-năng-sěuu ráan năi?
ร้านขายหนังสือร้านไหน

Which house?
bâan lăng năi?
บ้านหลังไหน

Which country do you like?
khun châwp bprà-thâed năi?
คุณชอบประเทศไหน
(bprà-thâed = country)

Which room?
hâwng năi?
ห้องไหน

Which bathroom?
hâwng-nám hâwng năi?
ห้องน้ำห้องไหน

Note the difference in the final two examples. The former has no classifier because it's the same as the object. The last has a classifier, even though the object and classifer are quite similar.

That

Several words are used in English as relative pronouns: *that, who, whom, whose* and *which*. *thêe* replaces all of these in Thai:

The man **who** I know.
phûu-chaai **thêe** phŏm rúu-jàk
ผู้ชายที่ผมรู้จัก

The restaurant **that** I go to eat with my friends.
ráan-aa-hăan **thêe** chăn bpai gin gàp phêuuan
ร้านอาหารที่ฉันไปกินกับเพื่อน

The hotel **which** he goes to swim at.
roong-raaem **thêe** khăo bpai wâai-nám
โรงแรมที่เขาไปว่ายน้ำ

The house **which** she bought.
bâan **thêe** ther séuu
บ้านที่เธอซื้อ

The person **who** bought my motorcycle.
khon **thêe** séuu ród maw-dter-sai khăwng-chăn
คนที่ซื้อรถมอเตอร์ไซค์ของฉัน

Let's look at some examples using *thêe* with *năi*. This most often occurs in questions to add extra information.

Which woman is it **that** you know?
phûu-yĭng khon **năi thêe** khun rúu-jàk?
ผู้หญิงคนไหนที่คุณรู้จัก

Here we are asking 'which woman?' The additional information is that 'it's the woman you know'. *thêe* joins them together.

Which chair is it that are you sitting in?
khun nâng thêe gâo-êe dtuua năi?
คุณนั่งที่เก้าอี้ตัวไหน

Which room do you sleep in?
khun nawn thêe hâwng năi?
คุณนอนที่ห้องไหน

Which car is it that you like?
ród khan năi thêe khun châwp?
รถคันไหนที่คุณชอบ

Which book would you like to buy at this shop?
khun yàak-jà séuu năng-sěuu lâem năi thêe ráan née?
คุณอยากจะซื้อหนังสือเล่มไหนที่ร้านนี้

'which' and 'that'

Chapter 18

Past tense

Let's first look at some short Thai sentences spoken in present tense and future tense. These are a mix of positive, negative and questions.

present

In present tense, most sentences have no time indicator.

You go.
khun bpai
คุณไป

He swims.
khăo wâai-nám
เขาว่ายน้ำ

Does he drink coffee?
khăo deùum gaa-faae măi?
เขาดื่มกาแฟไหม

We don't eat.
rao mâi gin
เราไม่กิน

She doesn't drink.
ther mâi deùum
เธอไม่ดื่ม

Do you like?
khun châwp măi?
คุณชอบไหม

future

As you know, changing these sentences to future tense is as easy as adding the word *jà*.

You **will** go.
khun jà bpai
คุณจะไป

He **will** swim.
khăo jà wâai-nám
เขาจะว่ายน้ำ

Will you wait for me?
khun jà raw chăn măi?
คุณจะรอฉันไหม

We **won't** eat.
rao jà mâi gin
เราจะไม่กิน

She **won't** drink.
ther jà mâi deùum
เธอจะไม่ดื่ม

Will she be ready?
ther jà phráwm măi?
เธอจะพร้อมไหม?

past (positive) 1

To form the past tense in positive sentences we just add the word *láeo*, meaning 'already'.

They **went**.
phûuak-khăo **bpai láeo**
พวกเขาไปแล้ว

We **ate**.
rao **gin láeo**
เรากินแล้ว

He **swam**.
khăo **wâai-nám láeo**
เขาว่ายน้ำแล้ว

She **drank**.
ther **deùum láeo**
เธอดื่มแล้ว

past (positive) 2

An alternative method is to also add the word *dâi* before the verb.

I **ate**.
chăn **dâi** gin láeo
ฉันได้กินแล้ว

He **walked**.
khăo **dâi** dern láeo
เขาได้เดินแล้ว

She **saw**.
ther **dâi** hĕn láeo
เธอได้เห็นแล้ว

I **spoke** with him.
chăn **dâi** phûud gàp khăo láeo
ฉันได้พูดกับเขาแล้ว

past (negative)

We use *mâi-dâi* without *láeo* to make negative past tense sentences.

I **didn't** eat.
chăn **mâi-dâi** gin
ฉันไม่ได้กิน

He **didn't** walk.
khăo **mâi-dâi** dern
เขาไม่ได้เดิน

She **didn't** look.
ther **mâi-dâi** mawng
เธอไม่ได้มอง

I **didn't** speak with him.
chăn **mâi-dâi** phûud gàp khăo
ฉันไม่ได้พูดกับเขา

past (questions)

A past tense question is made by adding the question word *rĕuu* (or) at the end of a past tense statement.

Did she eat?
ther gin láeo **rĕuu**?
เธอกินแล้วหรือ

Did he walk?
khăo dern láeo **rĕuu**?
เขาเดินแล้วหรือ

Did he leave?
khăo bpai láeo **rĕuu**?
เขาไปแล้วหรือ

Did she wait for you?
ther raw khun láeo **rĕuu**?
เธอรอคุณแล้วหรือ

The colloquial pronunciation for *rĕuu* in this usage is *rĕr*.

past simple precise

Just as with future tense, adding a time modifier allows us to be more precise. Note that if a 'time word' is included, we no longer need *láeo*.

He went **this morning**.
khăo bpai **dtawn-cháo-née**
เขาไปตอนเช้านี้

She didn't read it yesterday.
ther mâi-dâi àan mêuua-waan-née
เธอไม่ได้อ่านเมื่อวานนี้

We met him last week.
rao jer khăo aa-thíd thêe-láeo
เราเจอเขาอาทิตย์ที่แล้ว

They didn't buy it last month.
phûuak-khăo mâi-dâi séuu deuuan thêe-láeo
พวกเขาไม่ได้ซื้อเดือนที่แล้ว

Was she here yesterday?
ther yùu thêe-nêe mêuua-waan măi?
เธออยู่ที่นี่เมื่อวานไหม

present, future & past tense

another use of *láeo*

Although we take *láeo* to mean 'already', putting actions in the past, we can also use it alongside *jà*, like this:

I'm leaving now.
phŏm **jà** bpai **láeo**
ผมจะไปแล้ว

We're going to eat.
rao jà gin khâao láeo
เราจะกินข้าวแล้ว

In this instance, *jà* tells us it's a future action and *láeo* tells us it's about to happen.

exceptions

There are some exceptions when using *láeo* with *bpai* and *maa*. In this case we end up with something like present perfect tense.

gone

When *láeo* is used in conjunction with *bpai* it means that a person has gone somewhere and *is still there*.

He has **gone** to Bangkok. (and he is still there)
khăo **bpai** grung-thâep **láeo**
เขาไปกรุงเทพแล้ว

She has gone to school.
ther bpai roong-riian láeo
เธอไปโรงเรียนแล้ว

They have gone to England.
phûuak-khăo bpai ang-grìd láeo
พวกเขาไปอังกฤษแล้ว

They have gone to bed.
phûuak-khăo bpai nawn láeo
พวกเขาไปนอนแล้ว

been

When *maa* is included too it means that a person has been somewhere and returned.

The format is *bpai* + place (or action) + *maa*.

A time indicator can be included to show when the event took place.

I have **been** to eat. (but I am back now)
phŏm **bpai** gin **maa**
ผมไปกินมา

He has been to Bangkok.
khăo bpai grung-thâep maa
เขาไปกรุงเทพมา

She went to Phuket yesterday.
ther bpai phuu-gèd maa mêuua-waan
เธอไปภูเก็ตมาเมื่อวาน

I have been to the airport today.
chăn bpai sà-năam-bin maa wan-née
ฉันไปสนามบินมาวันนี้

We have been to Malaysia and Singapore.
rao bpai maa-laeh láe sĭng-khá-bpoo maa
เราไปมาเลย์และสิงคโปร์มา

I have been to work.
chăn bpai tham-ngaan maa
ฉันไปทำงานมา

We have been to eat breakfast.
rao bpai gin aa-hăan-cháo maa
เราไปกินอาหารเช้ามา

Where have you been?
khun bpai (thêe) năi maa?
คุณไป(ที่)ไหนมา

láeo, exceptions

more questions

---

not yet
yang
ยัง

We can also ask if something has *finished* or *been done* yet, by adding *yang* to the end of the question. Let's compare:

Did she eat**?**
ther gin **láeo rĕuu?**
เธอกินแล้วหรือ

Has she eaten **already?**
ther gin (láeo) **rĕuu-yang?**
เธอกิน(แล้ว)หรือยัง
(*láeo* can be ommitted)

Here are some example questions.

Have you eaten yet?
khun gin rĕuu-yang?
คุณกินหรือยัง

Has he come yet?
khăo maa rĕuu-yang?
เขามาหรือยัง

Have you met Peter yet?
khun jer Peter rĕuu-yang?
คุณเจอปีเตอร์หรือยัง

Has he spoken with you yet?
khăo phûud gàp khun rĕuu-yang?
เขาพูดกับคุณหรือยัง

Have you switched on the air-conditioner yet?
khun bpèrd aae rĕuu-yang?
คุณเปิดแอร์หรือยัง

Have you read this book yet?
khun àan năng-sĕuu lâem née rĕuu-yang?
คุณอ่านหนังสือเล่มนี้หรือยัง

can? questions

We can include the word *dâi* to make it a *can you ...... yet?* question.

Can you speak Thai **yet?**
khun phûud phaa-săa thai **dâi rĕuu-yang?**
คุณพูดภาษาไทยได้หรือยัง

Can she do it yet?
ther tham dâi rĕuu-yang?
เธอทำได้หรือยัง

Can I switch it on yet?
chăn bpèrd man dâi rĕuu-yang?
ฉันเปิดมันได้หรือยัง

Can you drive yet?
khun khàp ród dâi rĕuu-yang?
คุณขับรถได้หรือยัง

Can she speak English yet?
ther phûud phaa-săa ang-grìd dâi rĕuu-yang?
เธอพูดภาษาอังกฤษได้หรือยัง

All these questions are answered by repeating the verb with *láeo* for a positive answer, or replying *yang* for negative. (Remember: *dâi?* questions must be answered with *dâi* or *mâi-dâi*)

Question	**Yes**	**No**
gin khâao rĕuu-yang?	gin láeo	yang (yang-mâi-dâi gin)
rao bpai dâi rĕuu-yang?	bpai dâi	yang (yang bpai mâi-dâi)
àan năng-sĕuu rĕuu-yang?	àan láeo	yang (yang-mâi-dâi àan)

We can also ask about condition using adjectives:

Is it **hot yet**?
man **ráwn rěuu-yang**?
มันร้อนหรือยัง

Is the shop open yet?
ráan bpèrd rěuu-yang?
ร้านเปิดหรือยัง

Is the bar closed yet?
baa bpìd rěuu-yang?
บาร์ปิดหรือยัง

These questions can be answered with the adjective as usual.

Question	**Yes**	**No**
man ráwn rěuu-yang?	ráwn láeo	yang (yang-mâi ráwn)
ráan bpèrd rěuu-yang?	bpèrd láeo	yang (yang-mâi bpèrd)
baa bpìd rěuu-yang?	bpìd láeo	yang (yang-mâi bpìd)

not yet

or

---

or
rěuu
หรือ

In the questions above, *rěuu* is used with *yang* to ask 'or not yet?'. More commonly we use it to offer an option/alternative. If we include *rěuu* in a question, the option itself acts as the question, so the question word *mǎi?* is not needed.

Do you want coffee **or** tea?
khun yàak dâi gaa-faae **rěuu** chaa?
คุณอยากได้กาแฟหรือชา

I don't know if I should buy it **or** not.
mâi rúu wâa khuuan séuu **rěuu** mâi
ไม่รู้ว่าควรซื้อหรือไม่

láeo, exceptions

Chapter 19

Comparing

There are many ways to compare things in Thai. We'll cover the most common ones in this chapter.

the same	
alike, the same mĕuuan-gan เหมือนกัน	the same as mĕuuan เหมือน

We use *mĕuuan* to say one thing *resembles*, is *similar to* or *like* another thing, or that *it's not*. It is used to compare characteristics (size, colour, etc.). There is a difference between *the same* and *the same as*:

To say *the same*, we use *mĕuuan-gan*

To say *like* or *the same as*, we use *mĕuuan*

The houses in this village are **the same**.
bâan nai mùu-bâan née **mĕuuan-gan**
บ้านในหมู่บ้านนี้เหมือนกัน
(in = nai)

That shirt is **the same as** the one I bought last week.
sêuua dtuua nán **mĕuuan** thêe phŏm séuu aa-thíd thêe-láeo
เสื้อตัวนั้นเหมือนที่ผมซื้ออาทิตย์ที่แล้ว

You didn't do it **like** you said.
khun mâi-dâi tham **mĕuuan** thêe khun bàwk
คุณไม่ได้ทำเหมือนที่คุณบอก

Your shirt is **not the same as** mine.
sêuua khăwng-khun **mâi mĕuuan** khăwng-phŏm
เสื้อของคุณไม่เหมือนของผม

These two cars are **not the same** colour.
ród săwng khan née sĕe **mâi mĕuuan-gan**
รถสองคันนี้สีไม่เหมือนกัน

Do it **like** last time.
tham **mĕuuan** khráng thêe-láeo
ทำเหมือนครั้งที่แล้ว

the same as

---

the same
diaao-gan
เดียวกัน

We use *diaao-gan* to when we are talking about *one and the same* person, place or thing.

Peter and Jane live in Phuket. They live in the **same place**.
Peter láe Jane yùu thêe phuu-gèd. phûuak-khăo yùu **thêe diaao-gan**
ปีเตอร์และเจนอยู่ที่ภูเก็ต พวกเขาอยู่ที่เดียวกัน

That is the **same man** we saw yesterday.
nân kheuu **phûu-chaai khon diaao-gan** thêe rao hĕn mêuua-waan
นั่นคือผู้ชายคนเดียวกันที่เราเห็นเมื่อวาน

Is that the **same dog** you had last year?
nân bpen **măa dtuua diaao-gan** thêe khun mee bpee-thêe-láeo măi?
นั่นเป็นหมาตัวเดียวกันที่คุณมีปีที่แล้วไหม

That is **not the same woman** who came this morning.
nân **mâi châi phûu-yĭng khon diaao-gan** thêe maa dtawn-cháo née
นั่นไม่ใช่ผู้หญิงคนเดียวกันที่มาตอนเช้านี้

Is it the **same car**?
bpen **ród khan diaao-gan** măi?
เป็นรถคันเดียวกันไหม

I can't swim and speak at the **same time**.
phŏm wâai-nám láe phûud nai **waeh-laa diaao-gan** mâi-dâi
ผมว่ายน้ำและพูดในเวลาเดียวกันไม่ได้

We went to school on the **same day**.
rao bpai roong-riian **wan diaao-gan**
เราไปโรงเรียนวันเดียวกัน

the same

different

different dtàaek-dtàang แตกต่าง	differ dtàang ต่าง

These words can be used interchangeably.

Both *dtàaek-dtàang* and *dtàang* can be combined with *jàak* (from), *gàp* (with) and *gan* (each other, together).

dtàaek-dtàang jàak - different to/from

dtàang jàak - not the same as

dtàaek-dtàang gàp - different to/from

dtàang gàp - not the same as

dtàaek-dtàang gan - different to each other

dtàang gan - not the same as each other

This house is **different to** the one we looked at yesterday.
bâan lăng née **dtàaek-dtàang jàak** bâan thêe rao duu mêuua-waan
บ้านหลังนี้แตกต่างจากบ้านที่เราดูเมื่อวาน

Samui is **no different from** Phuket.
sà-mŭi **mâi dtàang gàp** phuu-gèd
สมุยไม่ต่างกับภูเก็ต

Thai people and British people are **different** (to each other).
khon thai láe khon ang-grìd **dtàang gan**
คนไทยและคนอังกฤษต่างกัน

Peter and John think **differently** (to each other).
Peter gàp John khíd **dtàang gan**
ปีเตอร์กับจอห์นคิดต่างกัน

These four chairs **aren't different** (to each other).
gâo-êe sèe dtuua née **mâi dtàang gan**
เก้าอี้สี่ตัวนี้ไม่ต่างกัน

That's **different from** what you said yesterday.
nân **dtàang jàak** thêe khun bàwk mêuua-waan
นั่นต่างจากที่คุณบอกเมื่อวาน

How are they **different** (from each other)?
man **dtàaek-dtàang gan** yàang-rai?
มันแตกต่างกันอย่างไร

What is different?
mee à-rai **dtàang gan**?
มีอะไรต่างกัน

Nothing is **different**.
mâi mee à-rai **dtàaek-dtàang**
ไม่มีอะไรแตกต่าง

different

-er and -est

-er	-est
gwàa	thêe-sùd
กว่า	ที่สุด

We use *gwàa* and *thêe-sùd* with adjectives to form a comparative or superlative. Let's introduce some new vocabulary to work with.

adjectives

good
dee
ดี

cheap
thùuk
ถูก

expensive
phaaeng
แพง

near
glâi
ใกล้

far
glai
ไกล

beautiful, pretty
sŭuai
สวย

difficult
yâak
ยาก

easy
ngâai
ง่าย

tasty, delicious
à-ròy
อร่อย

interesting
nâa-sŏn-jai
น่าสนใจ

fun
sà-nùk
สนุก

a little
nóy
น้อย

This is pretty straightforward - we just add the suffix after the adjective, like this:

adjective	**comparative**	**superlative**	
hot	hott**er**	hott**est**	
ráwn	ráwn **gwàa**	ráwn	**thêe-sùd**
ร้อน	ร้อนกว่า	ร้อนที่สุด	
little	less	least	
nóy	nóy gwàa	nóy	thêe-sùd
น้อย	น้อยกว่า	น้อยที่สุด	
good	better	best	
dee	dee-gwàa	dee	thêe-sùd
ดี	ดีกว่า	ดีที่สุด	

examples

Today is **hotter** than yesterday.
wan-née **ráwn gwàa** mêuua-waan
วันนี้ร้อนกว่าเมื่อวาน

This computer is **faster** and **cheaper** than that one.
khawm-piw-dtêr khrêuuang née **rew gwàa** láe **thùuk gwàa** khrêuuang nán
คอมพิวเตอร์เครื่องนี้เร็วกว่าและถูกกว่าเครื่องนั้น

This blouse is prettier than that one.
sêuua dtuua née sŭuai gwàa dtuua nán
เสื้อตัวนี้สวยกว่าตัวนั้น

Their house is the **biggest**.
bâan khăwng-phûuak-khăo **yài thêe-sùd**
บ้านของพวกเขาใหญ่ที่สุด

Which table is nearest the window?
dtóe dtuua năi yùu glâi gàp nâa-dtàang thêe-sùd?
โต๊ะตัวไหนอยู่ใกล้กับหน้าต่างที่สุด

My house is nearer than yours.
bâan khăwng-chăn yùu glâi gwàa bâan khăwng-khun
บ้านของฉันอยู่ใกล้กว่าบ้านของคุณ

That one is good, that one is better, but this one is the best.
an nán dee, an nán dee-gwàa, dtàae an née dee thêe-sùd
อันนั้นดี อันนั้นดีกว่า แต่อันนี้ดีที่สุด

This plate is the most delicious.
jaan née à-ròy thêe-sùd
จานนี้อร่อยที่สุด

This book is more interesting than yours.
năng-sěuu lâem née nâa-sŏn-jai gwàa khăwng-khun
หนังสือเล่มนี้น่าสนใจกว่าของคุณ

Phuket is more expensive than Bangkok, but more fun.
phuu-gèd phaaeng gwàa grung-thâep, dtàae sà-nùk gwàa
ภูเก็ตแพงกว่ากรุงเทพแต่สนุกกว่า

-er and -est

very, too

very, more	too
mâak	gern-bpai
มาก	เกินไป

We use *mâak* and *gern-bpai* to express degree. They can also be used together to express a greater degree.

The water is **very** hot.
nám ráwn **mâak**
น้ำร้อนมาก

The water is **not very** hot.
nám **mâi** ráwn **mâak**
น้ำไม่ร้อนมาก

The water is **too** hot.
nám ráwn **gern-bpai**
น้ำร้อนเกินไป

The water is **much too** hot.
nám ráwn **mâak gern-bpai**
น้ำร้อนมากเกินไป

It is very small.
man lék mâak
มันเล็กมาก

It is not very small.
man mâi lék mâak
มันไม่เล็กมาก

It is too small.
man lék gern-bpai
มันเล็กเกินไป

It is much too small.
man lék mâak gern-bpai
มันเล็กมากเกินไป

I can't do it, it's too difficult.
phŏm tham mâi-dâi, man yâak gern-bpai
ผมทำไม่ได้ มันยากเกินไป

This food is very tasty.
aa-hăan née à-ròy mâak
อาหารนี้อร่อยมาก

We can't walk to the hotel. It's much too far.
rao dern bpai roong-raaem mâi-dâi, man glai mâak gern-bpai
เราเดินไปโรงแรมไม่ได้ มันไกลมากเกินไป

I won't buy this car. It's too small and very expensive.
phŏm jà mâi séuu ród-yon khan née man lék gern-bpai láe phaaeng mâak
ผมจะไม่ซื้อรถยนต์คันนี้ มันเล็กเกินไปและแพงมาก

I know Peter well but Jane is a better friend.
phŏm rúu-jàk Peter dee dtàae Jane bpen phêuuan thêe dee-gwàa
ผมรู้จักปีเตอร์ดี แต่เจนเป็นเพื่อนที่ดีกว่า

mâak can also express degree with verbs and adverbs, like this:

We went **very late**.
rao bpai **cháa mâak**
เราไปช้ามาก

Jane runs very fast.
Jane wîng rew mâak
เจนวิ่งเร็วมาก

He talks a lot.
khăo phûud mâak
เขาพูดมาก

I love you very much.
chăn rák khun mâak
ฉันรักคุณมาก

I really like eating pizza.
phŏm châwp gin phíd-sâa mâak
ผมชอบกินพิซซ่ามาก

She likes him a lot.
ther châwp khăo mâak
เธอชอบเขามาก

I would really like to read this book.
phŏm yàak àan năng-sĕuu lâem née mâak
ผมอยากอ่านหนังสือเล่มนี้มาก

Unlike adjectives, for verbs we can't use *gwàa* or *thêe-sùd* on their own to make comparisons. We use them preceded by *mâak*, like this.

Phuket is good, but where do you like **more**?
phuu-gèd dee dtàae khun châwp thêe-năi **mâak gwàa**?
ภูเก็ตดี แต่คุณชอบที่ไหนมากกว่า

Where do you like **most**?
khun châwp thêe-năi **mâak thêe-sùd**?
คุณชอบที่ไหนมากที่สุด

Peter sleeps more than he works.
Peter nawn mâak gwàa tham-ngaan
ปีเตอร์นอนมากกว่าทำงาน

Bangkok has more restaurants than Phuket.
grung-thâep mee ráan-aa-hăan mâak gwàa phuu-gèd
กรุงเทพมีร้านอาหารมากกว่าภูเก็ต

That one is interesting, but I like this one the most.
an nán nâa-sŏn-jai, dtàae chăn châwp an née mâak thêe-sùd
อันนั้นน่าสนใจ แต่ฉันชอบอันนี้มากที่สุด

I waited for you for more than an hour.
chăn raw khun mâak gwàa nèung chûua-moong
ฉันรอคุณมากกว่าหนึ่งชั่วโมง

very and too

Chapter 20

More quantifiers

In chapter 12 we introduced quantifiers for use with things that we can count and put a number to. In this chapter we'll look at quantifiers for uncountable items.

Examples of uncountable items are *food, water, rice, money*.

These quantifiers can also be used with countable nouns when we want to express an indeterminate number.

not a lot, not much mâi yér ไม่เยอะ	some bâang บ้าง	a lot, much yér เยอะ
very few, very little nóy mâak น้อยมาก	few, a little nóy น้อย	not a little mâi nóy ไม่น้อย

Peter has **a lot** of money, Jane has **some**, but I have **very little**.
Peter mee ngern **yér**, Jane mee **bâang**, dtàae chăn mee nóy **mâak**
ปีเตอร์มีเงินเยอะ เจนมีบ้าง แต่ฉันมีน้อยมาก

There **aren't a lot of** people here.
thêe-nêe khon **mâi yér**
ที่นี่คนไม่เยอะ

Patong has **more than a few** restaurants.
bpàa-dtawng mee ráan-aa-hăan **mâi nóy**
ป่าตองมีร้านอาหารไม่น้อย

Why did you buy **so much** food?
tham-mai khun séuu aa-hăan maa **yér**
ทำไมคุณซื้ออาหารมาเยอะ

Few people know about this shop.
nóy khon thêe rúu-jàk ráan née
น้อยคนที่รู้จักร้านนี้

Singapore has **very few** Thai restaurants.
sĭng-khá-bpoo mee ráan-aa-hăan thai **nóy mâak**
สิงคโปร์มีร้านอาหารไทยน้อยมาก

Did **a lot of** people come?
mee khon maa **yér** mǎi?
มีคนมาเยอะไหม

Do you want **a lot of** sugar?
ao nám-dtaan **yér** mǎi?
เอาน้ำตาลเยอะไหม

We can't ask 'how many?' for indeterminate quantities and uncountable items. We need to ask 'how much?' of something.

How much money do you have?
khun mee ngern **thâo-rài**?
คุณมีเงินเท่าไหร่

How much rice do you want?
ao khâao thâo-rài?
เอาข้าวเท่าไหร่

more quantifiers

A note on *bâang* and *baang*, which are often confused. Both are used to describe frequency or quantity.

While these two words both mean 'some', their tone and usage is different.

baang can't be used on its own (*baang* alone means 'thin').

baang (common tone) must be followed by a countable noun.

sometimes	some days	some things
baang-khráng	baang-wan	baang-yàang
บางครั้ง	บางวัน	บางอย่าง

bâang (falling tone) is used after an uncountable noun or verb.

There are some.	I have some money.	I run a bit.
mee bâang	chǎn mee ngern bâang	chǎn wîng bâang
มีบ้าง	ฉันมีเงินบ้าง	ฉันวิ่งบ้าง

Chapter 21

Must, necessary, should

must

must, have to, need to
dtâwng
ต้อง

In everyday conversation we use *dtâwng* to say *must, have to* and *need to*. It may be understood as an instruction, obligation or a suggestion, depending on the context.

This is the same word *dtâwng* used in *dtâwng-gaan*.

I **must** go now (I have to go now).
phŏm **dtâwng** bpai dtawn-née
ผมต้องไปตอนนี้

You **don't have to** speak.
khun **mâi-dtâwng** phûud
คุณไม่ต้องพูด

Do I **need to** go with him?
chăn **dtâwng** bpai gàp khăo măi?
ฉันต้องไปกับเขาไหม

Yes.
dtâwng *or* dtâwng bpai
ต้อง, ต้องไป

No.
mâi-dtâwng *or* mâi-dtâwng bpai
ไม่ต้อง, ไม่ต้องไป

You must call him today. (suggestion)
khun dtâwng thoo-hăa khăo wan-née
คุณต้องโทรหาเขาวันนี้

You will often here *jà* included for emphasis.

She **really must** go to the hospital. (obligation)
ther **jà dtâwng** bpai roong-phá-yaa-baan
เธอจะต้องไปโรงพยาบาล

must

necessary

---

necessary to
jam-bpen-dtâwng
จำเป็นต้อง

This is more formal than *dtâwng* and indicates necessity.

Jane is ill. She **needs to** see a doctor.
Jane mâi sà-baai. ther **jam-bpen-dtâwng** bpai hăa măw
เจนไม่สบาย เธอจำเป็นต้องไปหาหมอ
(visit, go to see = hăa, doctor = măw)

He can wait for us. It's not necessary to go right now.
khăo raw rao dâi. man mâi jam-bpen-dtâwng bpai dtawn-née
เขารอเราได้ มันไม่จำเป็นต้องไปตอนนี้

Peter has no money. He must sell his motorbike.
Peter mâi mee ngern. khăo jam-bpen-dtâwng khăai ród maw-dter-sai khăwng-khăo
ปีเตอร์ไม่มีเงิน เขาจำเป็นต้องขายรถมอเตอร์ไซค์ของเขา

As with *dtâwng*, *jà* may be included for a stronger meaning.

Do you **really need to** go there?
khun **jam-bpen-jà-dtâwng** bpai thêe-nân măi?
คุณจำเป็นจะต้องไปที่นั่นไหม

Yes.
jam-bpen
จำเป็น

No.
mâi-jam-bpen
ไม่จำเป็น

necessary

should

better to dee-gwàa ดีกว่า	should nâa-jà น่าจะ	ought to khuuan (jà) ควร (จะ)

While these three words have similar meaning, *dee-gwàa* is added to the end of a sentence to make a suggestion or ask advice, like this:

It's late. We'd **better** go home.
man dèuk láeo. rao glàb-bâan **dee-gwàa**
มันดึกแล้ว เรากลับบ้านดีกว่า
(return = glàb, go home = glàb-bâan)

Would it be better to go alone?
bpai khon diaao dee-gwàa mǎi?
ไปคนเดียวดีกว่าไหม

You'd better have breakfast before you go to work.
gin aa-hǎan-cháo gàwn bpai tham-ngaan dee-gwàa
กินอาหารเช้าก่อนไปทำงานดีกว่า
(before = gàwn)

Of the remaining two words, *nâa-jà* is less strong than *khuuan*. It can be used alone as *nâa*, but more often than not you will hear it as *nâa-jà*.

We **should** tell Peter we are leaving.
rao **nâa-jà** bàwk Peter wâa rao jà bpai láeo
เราน่าจะบอกปีเตอร์ว่าเราจะไปแล้ว

You should do better than this.
khun nâa-jà tham dee-gwàa née
คุณน่าจะทำดีกว่านี้

That's the boss's seat. You shouldn't really sit there.
nân bpen thêe-nâng khǎwng-hǔua-nâa. khun mâi nâa-jà nâng thêe nân
นั่นเป็นที่นั่งของหัวหน้า คุณไม่น่าจะนั่งที่นั่น
(seat = thêe-nâng, boss = hǔua-nâa)

khuuan is the strongest word to say should or ought to. It can be used with or without *jà*.

You **should** study more if you want to speak Thai.
khun **khuuan-jà** riian mâak gwàa née thâa khun dtâwng-gaan phûud phaa-sǎa thai
คุณควรจะเรียนมากกว่านี้ถ้าคุณต้องการพูดภาษาไทย
(if = thâa [chapter 24])

You should tell him before Jane does.
khun khuuan bàwk khăo gàwn Jane jà bàwk
คุณควรบอกเขาก่อนเจนจะบอก

I shouldn't have eaten so much.
phŏm mâi khuuan gin yér
ผมไม่ควรกินเยอะ

We ought to go home before it rains.
rao khuuan glàb-bâan gàwn fŏn jà dtòk
เราควรกลับบ้านก่อนฝนจะตก

We can add *dee-gwàa* for emphasis. Here's the same sentence:

We **really ought to** go home before it rains.
rao **khuuan** glàb-bâan gàwn fŏn jà dtòk **dee-gwàa**
เราควรกลับบ้านก่อนฝนจะตกดีกว่า

should

Chapter 22

Prepositions of place

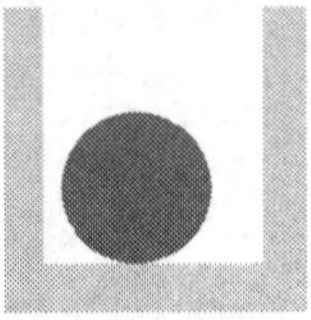

in / inside
nai / khâang-nai
ใน / ข้างใน

outside
khâang-nâwk
ข้างนอก

in front of
khâang-nâa
ข้างหน้า

behind
khâang-lăng
ข้างหลัง

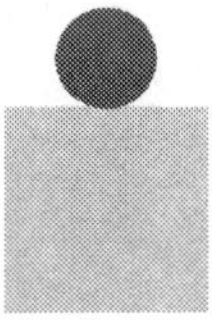

on
bon
บน

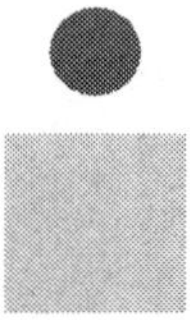

above
nĕuua
เหนือ

below / under
dtâi
ใต้

between
rá-wàang
ระหว่าง

across / opposite
dtrong-khâam
ตรงข้าม

beside
khâang-khâang
ข้าง ๆ

Just as in English, where we use 'side' (in → in*side*, out → out*side*), many of these words have or can have the word *khâang* attached to them.

As all these words are to do with position/location, we use them with the verb-to-be *yùu (thêe).*

Your book is **beside** you **on** the table.
năng-sěuu khăwng-khun yùu **khâang-khâang** khun **bon** dtóe
หนังสือของคุณอยู่ข้าง ๆ คุณบนโต๊ะ

The restaurant I like is **in** Bangla Road **across** from the coffee shop.
ráan-aa-hăan thêe phŏm châwp yùu **nai** soy baang-laa **dtrong-khâam** ráan-gaa-faae
ร้านอาหารที่ผมชอบ อยู่ในซอยบางลา ตรงข้ามร้านกาแฟ
(Bangla Road = soy baang-laa)

The shop I work at is **between** the police station and the hospital.
ráan thêe chăn tham-ngaan yùu **rá-wàang**
sà-thăa-nee dtam-rùuad gàp roong-phá-yaa-baan
ร้านที่ฉันทำงานอยู่ระหว่างสถานีตำรวจกับโรงพยาบาล

The cinema is **in** the shopping mall **above** the bank.
roong-năng yùu **nai** hâang **nĕuua** thá-naa-khaan
โรงหนังอยู่ในห้างเหนือธนาคาร

You can park **in** the car park **under** the shopping mall.
khun jàwd dâi **nai** laan-jàwd-ród **dtâi** hâang
คุณจอดได้ในลานจอดรถใต้ห้าง
(park = jàwd, car park = laan-jàwd-ród, mall [abbr.] = hâang)

It is hot **inside**. I will go **outside** and wait for you **in front** of the bakery.
khâang-nai ráwn phŏm jà bpai raw khun **khâang-nâwk nâa** ráan khăai khà-nŏm-bpang
ข้างในร้อน ผมจะไปรอคุณข้างนอก หน้าร้านขายขนมปัง
(bakery = ráan khăai khà-nŏm-bpang)

The shopping mall is **in front of** my house.
hâang-sàp-phá-sĭn-kháa yùu **nâa** bâan khăwng-chăn
ห้างสรรพสินค้าอยู่หน้าบ้านของฉัน
(shopping mall = hâang-sàp-phá-sĭn-kháa)

Where is the maid?
mâae-bâan yùu thêe-năi
แม่บ้านอยู่ที่ไหน
(maid = mâae-bâan)

She's **in** the kitchen.
ther yùu **nai** khruua
เธออยู่ในครัว
(kitchen = khruua)

The cat is **under** the table and the dog is **outside**, **behind** the house.
maaeo yùu **dtâi** dtóe láe măa yùu **khâang-nâwk** thêe **lăng** bâan
แมวอยู่ใต้โต๊ะและหมาอยู่ข้างนอก ที่หลังบ้าน

Half the coffee is **in** the cup and half is **on** the table!
gaa-faae khrêung nèung yùu **nai** thûuai láe khrêung nèung yùu **bon** dtóe
กาแฟครึ่งหนึ่งอยู่ในถ้วย และครึ่งหนึ่งอยู่บนโต๊ะ

There are six bottles of beer **on** the table **in** the kitchen.
mee biia hòk khùuad yùu **bon** dtóe **nai** khruua
มีเบียร์หกขวดอยู่บนโต๊ะ ในครัว

more prepositions of place

next door
khâang-bâan
ข้างบ้าน

in the middle
dtrong-glaang
ตรงกลาง

upstairs
khâang-bon
ข้างบน

downstairs
khâang-lâang
ข้างล่าง

new verbs

enter, go in
khâo
เข้า

exit, go out, leave
àwk
ออก

Enter the school.
khâo bpai nai roong-riian
เข้าไปในโรงเรียน

Exit the restaurant.
àwk jàak ráan-aa-hăan
ออกจากร้านอาหาร

He went upstairs with them.
khăo bpai khâang-bon gàp phûuak-khăo
เขาไปข้างบนกับพวกเขา

What is next door?
mee à-rai yùu khâang-bâan?
มีอะไรอยู่ข้างบ้าน

Is anybody downstairs?
mee khrai yùu khâang-lâang măi?
มีใครอยู่ข้างล่างไหม

I like to sit in the middle of the room.
chăn châwp nâng dtrong-glaang hâwng
ฉันชอบนั่งตรงกลางห้อง

prepositions of place

Prepositions of time

since dtâng-dtàae ตั้งแต่	until (jon) thĕung (จน)ถึง	from ... to ... jàak ... thĕung ... จาก ... ถึง ...
before gàwn ก่อน	when/during mêuua/dtawn เมื่อ/ตอน	after lăng (jàak) หลังจาก

since

dtâng-dtàae is used to refer to a past point in time until the present.

He hasn't come to work **since** Friday.
khăo mâi-dâi maa tham-ngaan **dtâng-dtàae** wan-sùk
เขาไม่ได้มาทำงานตั้งแต่วันศุกร์

She has been unwell since two hours ago.
ther mâi sà-baai dtâng-dtàae săwng chûua-moong thêe-láeo
เธอไม่สบายตั้งแต่สองชั่วโมงที่แล้ว

Peter has been out running since 8 a.m.
Peter àwk bpai wîng dtâng-dtàae bpàaed-moong-cháo
ปีเตอร์ออกไปวิ่งตั้งแต่แปดโมงเช้า

You've known since when?
khun rúu dtâng-dtàae mêuua-rài?
คุณรู้ตั้งแต่เมื่อไหร่

I haven't spoken to her since last year.
chăn mâi-dâi phûud gàp ther dtâng-dtàae bpee-thêe-láeo
ฉันไม่ได้พูดกับเธอตั้งแต่ปีที่แล้ว

until

(jon) thĕung is used to talk about now to a point in the future.

You must wait **until** Monday.
khun jà dtâwng raw **thĕung** wan-jan
คุณจะต้องรอถึงวันจันทร์

I will stay in Phuket until Saturday.
chăn jà yùu thêe phuu-gèd jon-thĕung wan-săo
ฉันจะอยู่ที่ภูเก็ตจนถึงวันเสาร์

We'll wait until she arrives.
rao jà raw jon-thĕung ther maa
เราจะรอจนถึงเธอมา

from ... to ...

He was busy **from** last month **until** yesterday.
khăo yûng **jàak** deuuan thêe-láeo **jon-thĕung** mêuua-waan
เขายุ่งจากเดือนที่แล้วจนถึงเมื่อวาน

The shop is open from 9 a.m. to 5 p.m.
ráan bpèrd jàak gâo-moong-cháo thĕung hâa-moong-yen
ร้านเปิดจากเก้าโมงเช้าถึงห้าโมงเย็น

Another way to say the same thing is to use *dtâng-dtàae* with *thĕung*.

Peter studies Thai from 1 p.m. until 3 p.m.
Peter riian phaa-săa thai dtâng-dtàae bàai-moong thĕung bàai-săam-moong
ปีเตอร์เรียนภาษาไทยตั้งแต่บ่ายโมงถึงบ่ายสามโมง

before

I will go **before** you.
phŏm jà bpai **gàwn** khun
ผมจะไปก่อนคุณ

He went to Bangkok before coming here.
khăo bpai grung-thâep gàwn maa thêe-nêe
เขาไปกรุงเทพก่อนมาที่นี่

You should tell him before she does.
khun khuuan bàwk khăo gàwn ther
คุณควรบอกเขาก่อนเธอ

when

I was here **when** he came.
chăn yùu thêe-nêe **mêuua** khăo maa
ฉันอยู่ที่นี่เมื่อเขามา

I walked when he was swimming.
phŏm dern dtawn khăo wâai-nám
ผมเดินตอนเขาว่ายน้ำ

Jane wasn't at home when we arrived.
Jane mâi-dâi yùu thêe bâan mêuua rao bpai-thĕung
เจนไม่ได้อยู่ที่บ้านเมื่อเราไปถึง
(arrive to = bpai-thĕung)

after

You came here **after** me.
khun maa thêe-nêe **lăng-jàak** chăn
คุณมาที่นี่หลังจากฉัน

I will go after lunch.
phŏm jà bpai lăng-jàak gin aa-hăan glaang-wan
ผมจะไปหลังจากกินอาหารกลางวัน

Jane likes to watch TV after dinner.
Jane châwp duu thee-wee lăng aa-hăan-yen
เจนชอบดูทีวีหลังอาหารเย็น

while/whilst/during

As a preposition of place we learned the word *rá-wàang*, meaning *between*. In a similar way, it can mean while/whilst/during as a preposition of time.

I will be in Phuket **during** the new year.
chăn jà yùu thêe phuu-gèd **rá-wàang** bpee mài
ฉันจะอยู่ที่ภูเก็ตระหว่างปีใหม่

He fell asleep while he was driving.
khăo làp bpai rá-wàang khàp ród
เขาหลับไประหว่างขับรถ

We stayed at home whilst it was raining.
rao yùu bâan rá-wàang fŏn dtòk
เราอยู่บ้านระหว่างฝนตก

prepositions of time

Chapter 23

Every, except, besides

every

---

every, each
thúk
ทุก

---

thúk is placed before the noun to which it refers:

I like **every** colour. (I like each colour.)
chăn châwp **thúk** sěe
ฉันชอบทุกสี

I like everyone here. (I like each person here.)
phŏm châwp thúk khon thêe-nêe
ผมชอบทุกคนที่นี่
(everyone/everybody = thúk khon)

Or between the noun and its classifier:

He likes to eat **every** kind of food.
khăo châwp gin aa-hăan **thúk** yàang
เขาชอบกินอาหารทุกอย่าง
(type, manner = yàang, everything = thúk-yàang)

He can drive every car.
khăo khàp ród thúk khan dâi
เขาขับรถทุกคันได้

Example sentences.

I want to see **everywhere** in Phuket.
chăn yàak bpai duu **thúk-thêe** nai phuu-gèd
ฉันอยากไปดูทุกที่ในภูเก็ต

The clothes in this shop are all nice.
sêuua-phâa ráan née sŭuai thúk dtuua
เสื้อผ้าร้านนี้สวยทุกตัว

We go to Singapore every year.
rao bpai sĭng-khá-bpoo thúk bpee
เราไปสิงค์โปร์ทุกปี

I eat rice every day.
chăn gin khâao thúk wan
ฉันกินข้าวทุกวัน

Every woman likes expensive things, but likes to buy cheap.
phûu-yĭng thúk khon châwp khăwng phaaeng, dtàae châwp séuu thùuk
ผู้หญิงทุกคนชอบของแพง แต่ชอบซื้อถูก
(things, stuff = khăwng, the same word we use as a possessive)

It's raining, everyone in the mall must wait to go home.
fŏn dtòk, thúk khon nai hâang dtâwng raw glàb-bâan
ฝนตก ทุกคนในห้างต้องรอกลับบ้าน

I eat fried rice every time I come to this restaurant.
chăn gin khâao phàd thúk khráng thêe maa ráan-aa-hăan née
ฉันกินข้าวผัดทุกครั้งที่มาร้านอาหารนี้
(stir-fry = phàd, fried rice = khâao phàd)

We can double the word *thúk* to mean 'each and every'.

There is a train to Bangkok **every single** day.
mee ród-fai bpai grung-thâep **thúk-thúk** wan
มีรถไฟไปกรุงเทพทุก ๆ วัน

The post office delivers each and every Monday.
bprai-sà-nee maa sòng khăwng thúk-thúk wan-jan
ไปรษณีย์มาส่งของทุก ๆ วันจันทร์
(deliver = sòng)

every

except

---

except
yók-wáen
ยกเว้น

---

yók-wáen is placed after the noun and immediately before the item it refers to.

I like every colour **except** red.
chăn châwp thúk sĕe **yók-wáen** sĕe-daaeng
ฉันชอบทุกสียกเว้นสีแดง

I like everybody here except him.
phŏm châwp thúk khon thêe-nêe yók-wáen khăo
ผมชอบทุกคนที่นี่ยกเว้นเขา

I like every kind except this.
chăn châwp thúk yàang yók-wáen nêe
ฉันชอบทุกอย่างยกเว้นนี่

We go to the market every day except Sunday.
phûuak-rao bpai dtà-làad thúk wan yók-wáen wan-aa-thíd
พวกเราไปตลาดทุกวันยกเว้นวันอาทิตย์

We can use *yók-wáen* along with *wâa* to say 'except that'.

I would like to live in Phuket, except that my work is in Bangkok.
chăn yàak yùu thêe phuu-gèd, yók-wáen wâa ngaan chăn yùu thêe grung-thâep
ฉันอยากอยู่ที่ภูเก็ตยกเว้นว่างานฉันอยู่ที่กรุงเทพ

I don't remember what he said **except that** he was going to Bangkok next week.
phŏm jam mâi-dâi wâa khăo phûud à-rai **yók-wáen wâa** khăo jà bpai grung-thâep aa-thíd-nâa
ผมจำไม่ได้ว่าเขาพูดอะไร ยกเว้นว่าเขาจะไปกรุงเทพอาทิตย์หน้า

except

besides

---

besides, apart from, other than
nâwk-jàak
นอกจาก

---

nâwk-jàak comes before the noun it refers to.

I don't swim anywhere **apart from** Patong beach.
phŏm mâi wâai-nám thêe-năi **nâwk-jàak** hàad bpàa-dtawng
ผมไม่ว่ายน้ำที่ไหนนอกจากหาดป่าตอง

Besides having no money, everything is good.
nâwk-jàak mâi mee ngern, thúk yàang dee
นอกจากไม่มีเงินทุกอย่างดี

Jane has no friends **other than** Peter.
Jane mâi mee phêuuan **nâwk-jàak** Peter
เจนไม่มีเพื่อนนอกจากปีเตอร์

besides

Chapter 24

If, then

if	then
thâa	gâw
ถ้า	ก็

We use 'if' to make conditional sentences. These are made up of a *main clause* and a *conditional clause* (the condition that may arise). The conditional clause can come before or after the main clause.

main clause	**conditional clause**
If you don't go now, **thâa** khun mâi bpai dtawn-née, ถ้าคุณไม่ไปตอนนี้	you will be late. khun jà săai คุณจะสาย
If we had a car, **thâa** rao mee ród, ถ้าเรามีรถ	we wouldn't need to walk. rao gâw mâi jam-bpen-dtâwng dern เราก็ไม่จำเป็นต้องเดิน

Now let's look at the same sentences with the clauses reversed.

conditional clause	**main clause**
You will be late khun jà săai คุณจะสาย	**if** you don't go now. **thâa** khun mâi bpai dtawn-née ถ้าคุณไม่ไปตอนนี้
We wouldn't need to walk rao mâi jam-bpen-dtâwng dern เราไม่จำเป็นต้องเดิน	**if** we had a car. **thâa** rao mee ród ถ้าเรามีรถ

As you can see, the meaning remains unchanged.

Some more examples.

If Peter goes, we can go with him.
thâa Peter bpai, rao bpai gàp khăo dâi
ถ้าปีเตอร์ไป เราไปกับเขาได้

I'll tell you **if** I see her.
jà bàwk khun **thâa** chăn hĕn ther
จะบอกคุณ ถ้าฉันเห็นเธอ

What will you do **if** Jane doesn't come?
khun jà tham yàang-rai **thâa** Jane mâi maa?
คุณจะทำอย่างไร ถ้าเจนไม่มา

If I don't do it, who will?
thâa phŏm mâi tham, khrai jà tham?
ถ้าผมไม่ทำ ใครจะทำ

We can include *gâw* to make an if/then sentence. *gâw* is used to link the two clauses.

If you eat too much, **then** you'll be ill.
thâa gin mâak gern-bpai, khun **gâw** jà mâi sà-baai
ถ้ากินมากเกินไปคุณก็จะไม่สบาย

If she wanted it, **then** she would buy it.
thâa ther dtâwng-gaan, ther **gâw** jà séuu
ถ้าเธอต้องการเธอก็จะซื้อ

If you do the shopping, **then** I'll do the cooking.
thâa khun séuu-khăwng, chăn **gâw** jà tham aa-hăan
ถ้าคุณซื้อของ ฉันก็จะทำอาหาร

---

then
láeo
แล้ว

We previously learned *láeo* as a past tense modifier. As a conjunction between two clauses it means 'then'.

We are going to Bangkok tomorrow, **then** next week we will go to Samui.
phrûng-née rao jà bpai grung-thâep **láeo** aa-thíd-nâa rao jà bpai sà-mŭi
พรุ่งนี้เราจะไปกรุงเทพ แล้วอาทิตย์หน้าเราจะไปสมุย

I'm going to swim then I'll have lunch.
phŏm jà wâai-nám láeo jà gin aa-hăan glaang-wan
ผมจะว่ายน้ำแล้วจะกินอาหารกลางวัน

if & then

Chapter 25

give, cause, allow, for

give, cause, allow, for
hâi
ให้

hâi is a very busy word in Thai, used in many different constructions to provide multiple meanings. We'll cover the most common usage in this chapter.

give

The simplest use of *hâi* is as the verb 'to give'.

The format is: giver + *hâi* + noun + recipient

Peter gave me money.
Peter hâi ngern chăn
ปีเตอร์ให้เงินฉัน

I gave the dog food.
phŏm hâi aa-hăan măa
ผมให้อาหารหมา

Jane gave me a ticket to go to Bangkok.
Jane hâi dtŭua chăn bpai grung-thâep
เจนให้ตั๋วฉันไปกรุงเทพ

give to

This is similar to 'give' above, except that we add the word *gàp* to mean 'to'. This is necessary when the noun is separated from the recipient by a classifier. Let's look at the difference.

Peter gave me a book.
Peter **hâi** năng-sěuu phŏm
ปีเตอร์ให้หนังสือผม

Peter gave me this book.
Peter **hâi** năng-sěuu lâem née **gàp** phŏm
ปีเตอร์ให้หนังสือเล่มนี้กับผม

Or it may be that the 'item' being given is very long, creating distance in the sentence between 'giver' and 'recipient'.

She **gave me** chicken, a plate of rice and a glass of water.
ther **hâi** gài, khâao nèung jaan láe nám nèung gâaeo **gàp chăn**
เธอให้ไก่ ข้าวหนึ่งจานและน้ำหนึ่งแก้วกับฉัน

let, allow

When *hâi* comes before a pronoun it means 'let', 'allow' or 'permit'.

She **let me** go to the bar alone.
ther **hâi phŏm** bpai baa khon diaao
เธอให้ผมไปบาร์คนเดียว

They let us come to Phuket.
phûuak-khăo hâi rao maa phuu-gèd
พวกเขาให้เรามาภูเก็ต

Will he let Jane drive?
khăo jà hâi Jane khàp măi?
เขาจะให้เจนขับไหม

We don't allow the dog to come in the house.
rao mâi hâi măa khâo maa nai bâan
เราไม่ให้หมาเข้ามาในบ้าน

Who let you turn on the fan?
khrai hâi khun bpèrd phád-lom?
ใครให้คุณเปิดพัดลม

You should let me do it.
hâi phŏm tham dee-gwàa
ให้ผมทำดีกว่า

to order, demand

The sentence form is the same as above, so this meaning is understood from context.

He made me do it.
khăo hâi chăn tham
เขาให้ฉันทำ

The boss told me to come here.
hŭua-nâa hâi phŏm maa thêe-nêe
หัวหน้าให้ผมมาที่นี่

They forced us to wait.
phûuak-khăo hâi rao raw
พวกเขาให้เรารอ

to make, to cause

Combining *tham* and *hâi* together changes the meaning to 'making something happen'.

This book **makes** me sad.
năng-sĕuu lâem née **tham-hâi** chăn sâo
หนังสือเล่มนี้ทำให้ฉันเศร้า
(sad = sâo)

The air-con makes the room cold very quickly.
aae tham-hâi hâwng yen rew mâak
แอร์ทำให้ห้องเย็นเร็วมาก

Running here made me hot.
wîng maa thêe-nêe tham-hâi phŏm ráwn
วิ่งมาที่นี่ทำให้ผมร้อน

to request

Combining *yàak* and *hâi* together changes the meaning to a request to do something.

I **want you to** speak with Peter.
chăn **yàak-hâi** khun phûud gàp Peter
ฉันอยากให้คุณพูดกับปีเตอร์

We don't want him to know.
rao mâi yàak-hâi khăo rúu
เราไม่อยากให้เขารู้

They want us to wait here.
phûuak-khăo yàak-hâi rao raw thêe-nêe
พวกเขาอยากให้เรารอที่นี่

All of the preceding ways to use *hâi* have been as a verb, but it can also act as the preposition 'for'.

for

By placing *hâi* before a pronoun, the meaning changes to 'for'.

I did this **for you**.
phŏm tham nêe **hâi khun**
ผมทำนี่ให้คุณ

She cooked for everyone.
ther tham-aa-hăan hâi thúk khon
เธอทำอาหารให้ทุกคน

Who are you buying that for?
khun séuu nân hâi khrai?
คุณซื้อนั่นให้ใคร

For Peter.
hâi Peter
ให้ปีเตอร์

Jane bought it for me.
Jane séuu hâi chăn
เจนซื้อให้ฉัน

with adjectives

hâi after a verb and before an adjective changes the meaning to an instruction.

Write **nicely**.
khĭian **hâi sŭuai**
เขียนให้สวย

Speak well.
phûud hâi dee
พูดให้ดี

Drive carefully.
khàp ród hâi dee
ขับรถให้ดี

hâi is used in many other ways too detailed to cover in this beginner's book. Listen out for *hâi* in conversation to see how others use it.

hâi

Chapter 26

Also, together

by, too, also	together	made of, made from
dûuai	dûuai-gan	tham-dûuai
ด้วย	ด้วยกัน	ทำด้วย

dûuai is another word which has more than one distinctly different meaning.

by, with

In this context, *dûuai* is used to say that something is done by an action or a noun.

Pizza is made **by** hand.
phíd-sâa tham dûuai meuu
พิซซ่าทำด้วยมือ
(hand(s) = meuu)

We write **with** a pen.
rao khĭian **dûuai** bpàak-gaa
เราเขียนด้วยปากกา

Jane went to Bangkok **by** car.
Jane bpai grung-thâep **dûuai** ród-yon
เจนไปกรุงเทพด้วยรถยนต์

too, also

A more common usage of *dûuai* is to say 'too', which can be used in many situations.

I would like some chicken, and **also** some rice.
phŏm yàak dâi gài láe khâao **dûuai**
ผมอยากได้ไก่และข้าวด้วย

If you go, I will go **too**.
thâa khun bpai, chăn jà bpai **dûuai**
ถ้าคุณไป ฉันจะไปด้วย

If I go, will you go **too**?
thâa chăn bpai, khun jà bpai dûuai măi?
ถ้าฉันไป คุณจะไปด้วยไหม

If you don't go, I won't go **either**.
thâa khun mâi bpai, chăn jà mâi bpai **dûuai**
ถ้าคุณไม่ไป ฉันจะไม่ไปด้วย

Alternatively, as we've already learned in chapters 19 & 24.

If you go, **then** I will go **too**.
thâa khun bpai, chăn **gâw** jà bpai **dûuai**
ถ้าคุณไป ฉันก็จะไปด้วย

If you don't go, **then** I won't go **either**.
thâa khun mâi bpai, chăn **gâw** jà mâi bpai **mĕuuan-gan**
ถ้าคุณไม่ไป ฉันก็จะไม่ไปเหมือนกัน

Either way is correct.

together

When *dûuai* is combined with *gan*, we have 'together'.

Peter and Jane go to Phuket **together**.
Peter láe Jane bpai phuu-gèd **dûuai-gan**
ปีเตอร์และเจนไปภูเก็ตด้วยกัน

We are learning Thai together.
rao riian phaa-săa thai dûuai-gan
เราเรียนภาษาไทยด้วยกัน

It's possible to drop the *dûuai* and just use *gan* on its own.

Want to see a movie (together)?
bpai duu năng **gan** măi?
ไปดูหนังกันไหม
(movie = năng)

Wait for Peter to come then we'll eat (together).
raw Peter maa láeo rao gin gan
รอปีเตอร์มา แล้วเรากินกัน

made of, made from

When *tham* is combined with *dûuai*, we have 'made of'.

This chair is **made of** wood.
gâo-êe dtuua née **tham-dûuai** mái
เก้าอี้ตัวนี้ทำด้วยไม้
(wood = mái)

What is this wardrobe **made from**?
dtûu-sêuua-phâa née **tham-dûuai** à-rai?
ตู้เสื้อผ้านี้ทำด้วยอะไร

dûuai

And then

---

and then
láeo-gâw
แล้วก็

This is a variation of *láeo* (chapter 24), again used to join two clauses in a sentence.

I am going to school, **and then** to the beach **and then** home.
chăn jà bpai roong-riian, **láeo-gâw** bpai hàad, **láeo-gâw** glàb-bâan
ฉันจะไปโรงเรียน แล้วก็ไปหาด แล้วก็กลับบ้าน

I must collect Peter at the airport, and then go to the hotel.
phŏm dtâwng bpai ráp Peter thêe sà-năam-bin láeo-gâw jà bpai roong-raaem
ผมต้องไปรับปีเตอร์ที่สนามบิน แล้วก็จะไปโรงแรม
(collect, receive = ráp)

You read the book first, and then I'll read it after.
khun àan năng-sĕuu gàwn láeo-gâw chăn àan thee-lăng
คุณอ่านหนังสือก่อน แล้วก็ฉันอ่านทีหลัง

She is a beautiful woman, and a nice person too.
ther bpen phûu-yĭng sŭuai láeo-gâw bpen khon dee dûuai
เธอเป็นผู้หญิงสวย แล้วก็เป็นคนดีด้วย

and then

May I have ...?, Could you ...?

May I have ...?	Could you ...?
khăw ...	khăw hâi ...
ขอ	ขอให้

We use *khăw* to request something or to get permission to do something. It is a polite way to make a request.

May I have a coffee please?
khăw gaa-faae nòy
ขอกาแฟหน่อย
(please = nòy)

This *nòy* is not the high tone word we learned meaning 'a little'. It is the most informal way to say 'please', pronounced low tone.

Can I have two more bottles of beer?
khăw biia èek săwng khùuad khráp
ขอเบียร์อีกสองขวดครับ

This request is made more polite by the addition of the masculine particle *khráp*.

May I sit here?
khăw nâng thêe-nêe dâi măi?
ขอนั่งที่นี่ได้ไหม

This 'can I?' request is made more polite by beginning the request with *khăw*.

Can I have ten more minutes?
khăw waeh-laa èek sìp naa-thee
ขอเวลาอีกสิบนาที

Can I have time to think please?
khăw waeh-laa khíd nòy (dâi măi?)
ขอเวลาคิดหน่อย(ได้ไหม)

We can use *khăw hâi* to politely request someone to do something.

Please take a seat and wait first.
khăw hâi nâng raw gàwn
ขอให้นั่งรอก่อน

Please drive slowly.
khăw hâi khàp cháa-cháa
ขอให้ขับช้า ๆ

What did he ask you to do?
khăo khăw hâi khun tham à-rai?
เขาขอให้คุณทำอะไร

May I have ...?

Chapter 27

Making nouns

a modifying prefix	a modifying prefix
khwaam-	gaan-
ความ-	การ-

khwaam

Using the prefix *khwaam,* we can change some verbs and adjectives into nouns. Most of these new words are abstract nouns or concepts, rather than actions. There are many everyday words which are prefixed with *khwaam*.

Let's look at the verbs and adjectives we already know first.

a thought, idea
khwaam-khíd
ความคิด
(from *think*)

knowledge
khwaam-rúu
ความรู้
(from *know*)

memory
khwaam-jam
ความจำ

love
khwaam-rák
ความรัก

understanding
khwaam-khâo-jai
ความเข้าใจ

cleanliness
khwaam-sà-àad
ความสะอาด

length
khwaam-yaao
ความยาว

width
khwaam-gwâang
ความกว้าง

height
khwaam-sǔung
ความสูง

heat
khwaam-ráwn
ความร้อน

beauty
khwaam-sǔuai
ความสวย

speed
khwaam-rew
ความเร็ว

necessity
khwaam-jam-bpen
ความจำเป็น

These are some useful new ones:

a dream
khwaam-făn
ความฝัน

truth
khwaam-jing
ความจริง

importance
khwaam-săm-khan
ความสำคัญ

happiness
khwaam-sùk
ความสุข

a secret
khwaam-láb
ความลับ

a mistake, error
khwaam-phìd
ความผิด

intention, determination
khwaam-dtâng-jai
ความตั้งใจ

feeling
khwaam-rúu-sèuk
ความรู้สึก

Example usage in sentences.

I don't know what to do. Do you have an idea?
phŏm mâi rúu jà tham à-rai, khun mee khwaam-khíd măi?
ผมไม่รู้จะทำอะไร คุณมีความคิดไหม

Peter has no knowledge of the Thai language.
Peter mâi mee khwaam-rúu phaa-săa thai
ปีเตอร์ไม่มีความรู้ภาษาไทย

I'm old. My memory is bad.
chăn gàae, khwaam-jam khăwng-chăn mâi dee
ฉันแก่ ความจำของฉันไม่ดี

The cleanliness of this restaurant is very good.
khwaam-sà-àad khăwng ráan-aa-hăan née dee mâak
ความสะอาดของร้านอาหารนี้ดีมาก

The car has a length of 4.5 metres and a width of 2.2 metres.
ród mee khwaam-yaao 4.5 máed láe khwaam-gwâang 2.2 máed
รถมีความยาว 4.5 เมตร และ ความกว้าง 2.2 เมตร

I have a need to go to Bangkok.
(It's a necessity that I go to Bangkok)
chăn mee khwaam-jam-bpen dtâwng bpai grung-thâep
ฉันมีความจำเป็นต้องไปกรุงเทพ

Beauty and cleanliness sometimes don't go together.
khwaam-sŭuai láe khwaam-sà-àad baang khráng mâi bpai dûuai-gan
ความสวยและความสะอาดบางครั้งไม่ไปด้วยกัน

I took the bullet train in Japan.
chăn nâng ród-fai khwaam-rew sŭung thêe yêe-bpùn
ฉันนั่งรถไฟความเร็วสูงที่ญี่ปุ่น

His dream has become reality.
khwaam-făn khăwng-khăo glaai bpen khwaam-jing
ความฝันของเขากลายเป็นความจริง
(to become, turn into = glaai)

The truth has great importance.
khwaam-jing mee khwaam-săm-khan mâak
ความจริงมีความสำคัญมาก

I have a feeling that you made a mistake.
chăn mee khwaam-rúu-sèuk wâa khun tham phìd
ฉันมีความรู้สึกว่าคุณทำผิด

If a mistake was made, then it was your mistake.
thâa tham phìd gâw bpen khwaam-phìd khăwng-khun
ถ้าทำผิด ก็เป็นความผิดของคุณ

Jane has a secret that she won't tell me.
Jane mee khwaam-láb thêe ther jà mâi bàwk chăn
เจนมีความลับที่เธอจะไม่บอกฉัน

I could see his determination when he spoke.
phŏm hĕn khwaam-dtâng-jai khăwng-khăo dtawn thêe khăo phûud
ผมเห็นความตั้งใจของเขาตอนที่เขาพูด

khwaam- prefix

gaan

gaan changes verbs in the same way as the gerund (-ing) in English. It is used with physical actions rather than concepts, for example, the verb 'to run' becomes 'running'. Look at the difference in these two sentences.

Jane **runs** every day.

Jane likes **running**.

In the first sentence, 'runs' is the verb.

In the second sentence, 'likes' is the verb and 'running' is the noun.

Again, we'll first look at the verbs we already know.

walking
gaan-dern
การเดิน

running
gaan-wîng
การวิ่ง

flying
gaan-bin
การบิน

speaking
gaan-phûud
การพูด

drinking
gaan-dèuum
การดื่ม

reading
gaan-àan
การอ่าน

writing
gaan-khǐian
การเขียน

There are hundreds of words which use the prefix *gaan*, because we can place it before any verb, but here are just a couple of the more useful ones.

education
gaan-sèuk-sǎa
การศึกษา

competition
gaan-khàaeng-khǎn
การแข่งขัน

having
gaan-mee
การมี

travelling
gaan-dern-thaang
การเดินทาง

Walking makes me feel good.
gaan-dern tham-hâi chǎn rúu-sèuk dee
การเดินทำให้ฉันรู้สึกดี

Education is very important.
gaan-sèuk-sǎa mee khwaam-sǎm-khan mâak
การศึกษามีความสำคัญมาก

Having money is a necessity.
gaan-mee ngern bpen sìng thêe jam-bpen
การมีเงินเป็นสิ่งที่จำเป็น
(a thing = sìng, alternatively *sìng khǎwng*)

Running is something I do but don't enjoy.
gaan-wîng bpen sìng thêe chăn tham dtàae mâi sà-nùk
การวิ่งเป็นสิ่งที่ฉันทำแต่ไม่สนุก

Flying is faster than driving.
gaan-bin rew gwàa gaan-khàp
การบินเร็วกว่าการขับ

Drinking too much beer is bad for health.
gaan-dèuum biia mâak gern-bpai mâi dee dtàw sùk-khà-phâap
การดื่มเบียร์มากเกินไปไม่ดีต่อสุขภาพ
(to, for, against = dtàw, health = sùk-khà-phâap)

Reading is necessary in education.
gaan-àan bpen sìng jam-bpen nai gaan-sèuk-săa
การอ่านเป็นสิ่งจำเป็นในการศึกษา

The competition is open to everyone.
gaan-khàaeng-khăn bpèrd hâi thúk khon
การแข่งขันเปิดให้ทุกคน

Writing a book is more difficult than reading one.
gaan-khĭian năng-sěuu yâak gwàa gaan-àan
การเขียนหนังสือยากกว่าการอ่าน

Travelling is fun but expensive.
gaan-dern-thaang sà-nùk dtàae phaaeng
การเดินทางสนุกแต่แพง

gaan- prefix

used with *bpen*

khwaam-bpen and *gaan-bpen* both mean 'being'. The former refers to a 'state of being', while the latter means it is an 'ongoing quality'. Keep in mind that *khwaam* relates to concepts.

Consider these differences:

There is a possibility that electric cars will sell well.
mee khwaam-bpen-bpai-dâi thêe ród-yon fai-fáa jà khăai dâi dee
มีความเป็นไปได้ที่รถยนต์ไฟฟ้าจะขายได้ดี
(electric, electricity = fai-fáa)

Being a man is sometimes difficult.
gaan-bpen-phûu-chaai baang-khráng gâw yâak
การเป็นผู้ชายบางครั้งก็ยาก

Chapter 28

Ever & frequency

ever	often	regularly
khaey	bòy	(bpen) bprà-jam
เคย	บ่อย	(เป็น)ประจำ

ever

We say 'used to', 'ever', 'never' and ask 'have/has .... ever?' using *khaey*.

khaey refers to things that happened in the past, so it also means 'at one time', 'once', etc.

Here's an example of each.

I **used to** run every morning.
phŏm **khaey** wîng thúk cháo
ผมเคยวิ่งทุกเช้า

Peter **once** lived in Singapore.
Peter **khaey** yùu thêe sĭng-khá-bpoo
ปีเตอร์เคยอยู่ที่สิงคโปร์

Jane **has never** been to Bangkok.
Jane **mâi khaey** bpai grung-thâep
เจนไม่เคยไปกรุงเทพ

Have you **ever** worked in a hotel?
khun **khaey** tham-ngaan roong-raaem **măi?**
คุณเคยทำงานโรงแรมไหม

We can answer *khaey* questions with a simple yes or no, like this:

Have you ever been to Bangkok?
khun khaey bpai grung-thâep măi?
คุณเคยไปกรุงเทพไหม

Yes, I **have**.
chăn **khaey** bpai
ฉันเคยไป

No, I **haven't** been **yet**.
chăn **yang-mâi khaey** bpai
ฉันยังไม่เคยไป

No, I have **never** been.
chăn mâi **khaey** bpai
ฉันไม่เคยไป

frequency

We can add extra information regarding the frequency that something happens, using a few words we already know.

how often ...?
... bòy thâo-rài
... บ่อยเท่าไหร่

how many times ...?
... gèe khráng
... กี่ครั้ง

xx times
xx khráng
xx ครั้ง

not often
mâi bòy
ไม่บ่อย

how many times ...?
... khaey ... gèe khráng
... เคย ... กี่ครั้ง

sometimes
baang-khráng
บางครั้ง

not many times
mâi gèe khráng
ไม่กี่ครั้ง

many times
lăai khráng
หลายครั้ง

Example sentences.

I go to Bangkok **often**.
chăn bpai grung-thâep **bòy**
ฉันไปกรุงเทพบ่อย

I go to Bangkok **regularly**.
chăn bpai grung-thâep bpen **bprà-jam**
ฉันไปกรุงเทพเป็นประจำ

I have been to Bangkok **four times**.
chăn khaey bpai grung-thâep **sèe khráng**
ฉันเคยไปกรุงเทพสี่ครั้ง

I have been to Bangkok **many times**.
chăn khaey bpai grung-thâep **lăai khráng**
ฉันเคยไปกรุงเทพหลายครั้ง

Have you **ever** eaten crab?
khun **khaey** gin bpuu **măi?**
คุณเคยกินปูไหม
(crab = bpuu)

I eat crab **very often**.
chăn gin bpuu **bòy mâak**
ฉันกินปูบ่อยมาก

Do you exercise **often?**
khun àwk-gam-lang-gaai **bòy măi?**
คุณออกกำลังกายบ่อยไหม
(exercise = àwk-gam-lang-gaai)

I exercise **every day**.
chăn àwk-gam-lang-gaai **thúk wan**
ฉันออกกำลังกายทุกวัน

How often do you swim?
khun wâai-nám **bòy thâo-rài?**
คุณว่ายน้ำบ่อยเท่าไหร่

I swim **every day**.
chăn wâai-nám **thúk wan**
ฉันว่ายน้ำทุกวัน

Have you **ever** been to see a movie at Central?
khun **khaey** bpai duu-năng thêe sen-thrân **măi?**
คุณเคยไปดูหนังที่เซ็นทรัลไหม

My husband and I go to see movies **very often**.
chăn gàp săa-mee bpai duu-năng **bòy mâak**
ฉันกับสามีไปดูหนังบ่อยมาก
(husband = săa-mee)

How often do you eat out?
khun àwk bpai gin khâao khâang-nâwk **bòy thâo-rài?**
คุณออกไปกินข้าวข้างนอกบ่อยเท่าไหร่

We eat out **twice per week**.
phûuak-rao gin khâao khâang-nâwk **aa-thíd lá săwng khráng**
พวกเรากินข้าวข้างนอกอาทิตย์ละสองครั้ง
(per, each = lá)

Do you study Thai **regularly?**
khun riian phaa-săa-thai bpen **bprà-jam măi?**
คุณเรียนภาษาไทยเป็นประจำไหม

I study at school **3 days per week**.
chăn riian thêe roong-riian **aa-thíd lá săam wan**
ฉันเรียนที่โรงเรียนอาทิตย์ละสามวัน

Have you **ever** been to Europe?
khun **khaey** bpai yú-ròop **măi?**
คุณเคยไปยุโรปไหม

We go to Europe **every year**. **Some years** we go **twice**.
phûuak-rao bpai yú-ròop **thúk bpee, baang-bpee** rao bpai **săwng khráng**
พวกเราไปยุโรปทุกปี บางปีเราไปสองครั้ง

Do you study Thai **every day?**
khun riian phaa-săa-thai **thúk wan măi?**
คุณเรียนภาษาไทยทุกวันไหม

I study **regularly**, but **some days** I don't study.
chăn riian bpen **bprà-jam**, dtàae **baang-wan** mâi riian
ฉันเรียนเป็นประจำ แต่บางวันไม่เรียน

Have you **ever** visited Hadyai?
khun **khaey** bpai thîaao hàad-yài **măi?**
คุณเคยไปเที่ยวหาดใหญ่ไหม
(travel, tour = thîaao)

I **haven't** been to Hadyai **yet**.
chăn **yang mâi khaey** bpai thîaao hàad-yài
ฉันยังไม่เคยไปเที่ยวหาดใหญ่

Peter **often** cooks dinner for Jane.
Peter tham aa-hăan-yen hâi Jane **bòy**
ปีเตอร์ทำอาหารเย็นให้เจนบ่อย

Some new words relating to frequency. This table shows how they relate to one another.

0%	>	>	>	>	100%
never	rarely	sometimes	often	usually	always
mâi khaey	mâi bòy	baang khráng	bòy	mák-jà	sà-mĕr
ไม่เคย	ไม่บ่อย	บางครั้ง	บ่อย	มักจะ	เสมอ

always

always (constantly)
sà-mĕr
เสมอ

all the time (during)
dtà-làwd
ตลอด

always (on and on)
rêuuai-rêuuai
เรื่อย ๆ

These first three have subtle differences which are best explained through examples.

sà-mĕr is used with actions that go on constantly, unchanging.

It's **always** hot in Phuket.
phuu-gèd ráwn **sà-mĕr**
ภูเก็ตร้อนเสมอ

Monday always comes before Tuesday.
wan-jan maa gàwn wan-ang-khaan sà-mĕr
วันจันทร์มาก่อนวันอังคารเสมอ

sà-mĕr can also be used with things that can *possibly* be constant.

He **always** works hard.
khăo tham-ngaan nàk **sà-mĕr**
เขาทำงานหนักเสมอ
(work hard = work heavy = tham-ngaan nàk)

Mary always comes late.
Mary maa săai sà-mĕr
แมรี่มาสายเสมอ

The train always leaves at 3 a.m.
ród-fai àwk dtawn dtee-săam sà-mĕr
รถไฟออกตอนตีสามเสมอ

When I ask him, he always answers the same.
mêuua phŏm thăam khăo, khăo dtàwp mĕuuan-gan sà-mĕr
เมื่อผมถามเขา เขาตอบเหมือนกันเสมอ

We use *rêuuai-rêuuai* to say that something goes on and on, continuously.

He never stops eating. He eats **all the time** (constantly).
khăo mâi khaey yùd gin, khăo gin **rêuuai-rêuuai**
เขาไม่เคยหยุดกิน เขากินเรื่อย ๆ
(stop = yùd)

The maid works non-stop until late afternoon.
mâae-bâan tham-ngaan rêuuai-rêuuai jon-thĕung dtawn-yen
แม่บ้านทำงานเรื่อย ๆ จนถึงตอนเย็น

dtà-làwd is used to say that something happens for a duration, throughout a period of time.

I waited an hour for him. He was in the bar **the whole time**.
chăn raw khăo nèung chûua-moong, khăo yùu nai baa **dtà-làwd waeh-laa**
ฉันรอเขาหนึ่งชั่วโมง เขาอยู่ในบาร์ตลอดเวลา

Peter has lived in Singapore his entire life.
Peter yùu thêe sĭng-khá-bpoo dtà-làwd chee-wíd
ปีเตอร์อยู่ที่สิงคโปร์ตลอดชีวิต
(chee-wíd = life)

Must you work all day and night?
khun dtâwng tham-ngaan dtà-làwd wan dtà-làwd kheuun măi?
คุณต้องทำงานตลอดวันตลอดคืนไหม

usually

usually, often mák-jà มักจะ	usually, normally bpòk-gà-dtì ปกติ

These two words are quite interchangeable and can also be used together in a sentence.

School is **usually** closed on Sunday.
roong-riian **mák-jà** bpìd wan-aa-thíd
โรงเรียนมักจะปิดวันอาทิตย์

He usually stays home at the weekend.
khăo mák-jà yùu bâan săo-aa-thíd
เขามักจะอยู่บ้านเสาร์อาทิตย์
(weekend = săo-aa-thíd)

Both sentences could equally be written:

School is **usually** closed on Sunday.
bpòk-gà-dtì roong-riian jà bpìd wan-aa-thíd
ปกติโรงเรียนจะปิดวันอาทิตย์

He usually stays at home at the weekend.
bpòk-gà-dtì khăo jà yùu bâan săo-aa-thíd
ปกติเขาจะอยู่บ้านเสาร์อาทิตย์
(weekend = săo-aa-thíd)

Or even using both words:

School is **usually** closed on Sunday.
bpòk-gà-dtì roong-riian **mák-jà** bpìd wan-aa-thíd
ปกติโรงเรียนมักจะปิดวันอาทิตย์

We can say that something is *unusual*.

Today is **unusual**. I have a day off.
wan-née **mâi bpòk-gà-dtì**, chăn mee wan-yùd
วันนี้ไม่ปกติ ฉันมีวันหยุด
(day off = wan-yùd)

Unusual can also be expressed as *phìd-bpòk-gà-dtì*, where *phìd* means 'wrong'.

It's **very unusual** that Peter didn't have a coffee this morning.
cháo née **phìd-bpòk-gà-dtì mâak** thêe Peter mâi-dâi deùum gaa-faae
เช้านี้ผิดปกติมากที่ปีเตอร์ไม่ได้ดื่มกาแฟ

ever & frequency

Chapter 29

Maybe & Because

maybe	because
àad (jà)	phró (wâa)
อาจ(จะ)	เพราะ(ว่า)

àad-jà is used to say 'might', 'maybe', 'perhaps' and 'possibly'. You can leave out the *jà* if you wish.

I **might** not buy it **because** it's expensive.
chăn **àad-jà** mâi séuu phró man **phaaeng**
ฉันอาจจะไม่ซื้อเพราะมันแพง

I might be late home. You don't need to wait.
phŏm àad-jà glàb-bâan cháa, khun mâi jam-bpen-dtâwng raw
ผมอาจจะกลับบ้านช้า คุณไม่จำเป็นต้องรอ

It could be a table, it could be a chair.
àad-jà bpen dtóe, àad-jà bpen gâo-êe
อาจจะเป็นโต๊ะ อาจจะเป็นเก้าอี้

I'll take a look for you. He might not have gone out.
chăn jà duu hâi, khăo àad-jà mâi-dâi àwk bpai
ฉันจะดูให้ เขาอาจจะไม่ได้ออกไป

Peter might not have sold his house yet.
Peter àad-jà yang-mâi-dâi khăai bâan khăwng-khăo
ปีเตอร์อาจจะยังไม่ได้ขายบ้านของเขา

phró is a preposition used to introduce a reason.

I didn't buy it **because** it's expensive.
chăn mâi-dâi séuu **phró** man phaaeng
ฉันไม่ได้ซื้อเพราะมันแพง

They come to Phuket often **because** they like it here.
phûuak-khăo maa phuu-gèd bòy, **phró-wâa** phûuak-khăo châwp thêe-nêe
พวกเขามาภูเก็ตบ่อย เพราะว่าพวกเขาชอบที่นี่

Did you stay at home because of the rain?
khun yùu bâan phró fŏn dtòk châi măi?
คุณอยู่บ้านเพราะฝนตกใช่ไหม

We must book a room because we are going to Bangkok tomorrow.
rao dtâwng jawng hâwng, phró-wâa rao jà bpai grung-thâep phrûng-née
เราต้องจองห้อง เพราะว่าเราจะไปกรุงเทพพรุ่งนี้
(to book = jawng, book a room = jawng hâwng)

If you are not ready, I'll go alone because I have to be there at 3pm.
thâa khun mâi phráwm chăn jà bpai khon diaao phró-wâa chăn dtâwng yùu thêe-nân waeh-laa bàai săam
ถ้าคุณไม่พร้อม ฉันจะไปคนเดียว เพราะว่าฉันต้องอยู่ที่นั่นเวลาบ่ายสาม

I might not be able to go with you because I don't have any money.
chăn àad-jà bpai gàp khun mâi-dâi phró mâi mee ngern
ฉันอาจจะไปกับคุณไม่ได้เพราะไม่มีเงิน

maybe & because

Chapter 30

Prefixes and suffixes

heart/mind
jai
ใจ

jai is used as both a prefix and suffix with many words related to emotions. For the prefixes, we'll provide the meaning of the separate words (in brackets) as well as the meaning of the new word as a whole. We feel it makes them easier to remember.

We'll start with the most useful prefixed words.

kind, nice, generous
jai-dee (good-hearted)
ใจดี

nasty, unkind
jai-dam (black-hearted)
ใจดำ

strongwilled
jai-khăeng (hard-hearted)
ใจแข็ง

weak, easily influenced
jai-àwn (soft-hearted)
ใจอ่อน

broad-minded
jai-gwâang (wide-hearted)
ใจกว้าง

narrow-minded
jai-khâaep (narrow-hearted)
ใจแคบ

calm, relaxed
jai-yen (cold-hearted)
ใจเย็น

hot-headed, rash
jai-ráwn (hot-hearted)
ใจร้อน

bold, brave
jai-glâa (brave-hearted)
ใจกล้า

sensitive, touchy
jai-nóy (small-hearted)
ใจน้อย

Next we have some suffixed *jai* words.

glad, happy
dee-jai
ดีใจ

unappreciated, feel slighted
nóy-jai
น้อยใจ

sorry, saddened
sĭia-jai
เสียใจ

willpower, motivation
gam-lang-jai
กำลังใจ

satisfied, pleased
phaw-jai
พอใจ

relaxed, happy
sà-baai-jai
สบายใจ

proud
phuum-jai
ภูมิใจ

shocked, surprised
dtòk-jai
ตกใจ

sentence examples

Peter is kind. He helps everyone.
Peter bpen khon jai-dee, khăo chûuai thúk khon
ปีเตอร์เป็นคนใจดี เขาช่วยทุกคน
(help, assist = chûuai)

I don't like Tom. He speaks badly and is not a nice person.
chăn mâi châwp Tom, khăo phûud mâi dee láe bpen khon jai-dam
ฉันไม่ชอบทอม เขาพูดไม่ดีและเป็นคนใจดำ

Jane is a strongwilled woman who works alone.
Jane bpen phûu-yĭng jai-khăeng thêe tham-ngaan khon diaao
เจนเป็นผู้หญิงใจแข็งที่ทำงานคนเดียว

Mary knows her father has a soft heart for her.
Mary rúu wâa phâw ther jai-àwn gàp ther
แมรี่รู้ว่าพ่อเธอใจอ่อนกับเธอ

Peter is cool-headed and takes time to think.
Peter bpen khon jai-yen láe chái waeh-laa khíd
ปีเตอร์เป็นคนใจเย็นและใช้เวลาคิด

Jane is happy to have bought a new car.
Jane dee-jai thêe dâi séuu ród khan mài
เจนดีใจที่ได้ซื้อรถคันใหม่

I have no motivation to do anything.
chăn mâi mee gam-lang-jai jà tham à-rai
ฉันไม่มีกำลังใจจะทำอะไร

I'm not proud of my work, but I'm satisfied with it.
phŏm mâi phuum-jai nai ngaan khăwng-phŏm dtàae phŏm phaw-jai
ผมไม่ภูมิใจในงานของผม แต่ผมพอใจ

I'm sorry to hear he is unwell.
chăn sĭia-jai thêe dâi-yin wâa khăo mâi sà-baai
ฉันเสียใจที่ได้ยินว่าเขาไม่สบาย

I was shocked to see Jane swimming.
chăn dtòk-jai thêe hĕn Jane wâai-nám
ฉันตกใจที่เห็นเจนว่ายน้ำ

jai prefix and suffix

-worthy, -able, should
nâa-
น่า-

---

nâa is used to prefix verbs to make the suffixes '-able' and '-worthy'.

nâa is used as a helping verb to say 'should ...', 'ought to ...'.

We can use *nâa* to prefix many of the words we already know.

looks tasty (worth eating)
nâa-gin
น่ากิน

worth a look
nâa-duu
น่าดู

worth reading
nâa-àan
น่าอ่าน

cute, lovable
nâa-rák
น่ารัก

worth going
nâa-bpai
น่าไป

worth staying at/living at
nâa-yùu
น่าอยู่

interesting (from chapter 19)
nâa-sŏn-jai
น่าสนใจ

Here are some new verbs that this prefix is often used with.

pitiful
nâa-sŏng-săan
น่าสงสาร

scary
nâa-gluua
น่ากลัว

ugly, horrible
nâa-glìiad
น่าเกลียด

believable, convincing
nâa-chêuua
น่าเชื่อ

sentence examples

The fried rice looks very tasty!
khâao phàd duu nâa-gin mâak
ข้าวผัดดูน่ากินมาก

Your book looks interesting. Is it worth reading?
năng-sĕuu khăwng-khun duu nâa-sŏn-jai, man nâa-àan măi?
หนังสือของคุณดูน่าสนใจ มันน่าอ่านไหม

This movie looks like it's worth seeing.
năng rêuuang née nâa-duu
หนังเรื่องนี้น่าดู
(story = rêuuang [also classifier for movies])

Your dog is really cute.
măa khăwng-khun nâa-rák mâak
หมาของคุณน่ารักมาก

Bangkok is worth a visit, but not to live.
grung-thâep nâa-bpai dtàae mâi nâa-yùu
กรุงเทพน่าไปแต่ไม่น่าอยู่

He is very old and can't walk. He is pitiful.
khăo gàae mâak láe dern mâi-dâi khăo nâa-sŏng-săan
เขาแก่มากและเดินไม่ได้ เขาน่าสงสาร

Peter drives fast. It's very frightening.
Peter khàp ród rew man nâa-gluua mâak
ปีเตอร์ขับรถเร็ว มันน่ากลัวมาก

I don't like this sofa. It's horrible.
chăn mâi châwp soo-faa dtuua née man nâa-glìiad
ฉันไม่ชอบโซฟาตัวนี้ มันน่าเกลียด

I don't know what he told her, but it wasn't very believable.
phŏm mâi rúu wâa khăo bàwk à-rai gàp ther dtàae man mâi nâa-chêuua
ผมไม่รู้ว่าเขาบอกอะไรกับเธอ แต่มันไม่น่าเชื่อ

As we saw in chapter 21, using *nâa-* with *jà*, means should/ought to.

Your car is very old. You should buy a new one.
ród khăwng-khun gào mâak, khun nâa-jà séuu khan mài
รถของคุณเก่ามาก คุณน่าจะซื้อคันใหม่

You shouldn't eat before you swim.
mâi nâa-jà gin gàwn wâai-nám
ไม่น่าจะกินก่อนว่ายน้ำ

We should be able to get coffee here.
rao nâa-jà dâi gaa-faae thêe-nêe
เราน่าจะได้กาแฟที่นี่

You should go with her.
khun nâa-jà bpai gàp ther
คุณน่าจะไปกับเธอ

nâa- prefix

Chapter 31

In the past

a moment ago mêuua-gêe เมื่อกี้	just now phêrng เพิ่ง	not long ago mâi-naan-maa-née ไม่นานมานี้
recently, soon rew-rew-née เร็ว ๆ นี้	the other day wan-gàwn วันก่อน	a long time ago naan-maa-láeo นานมาแล้ว
in the past mêuua-gàwn เมื่อก่อน		

a moment ago

He's not here, he left **a moment ago**.
khăo mâi yùu, khăo àwk bpai **mêuua-gêe**
เขาไม่อยู่ เขาออกไปเมื่อกี้

I can't find my phone. I saw it a moment ago.
chăn hăa meuu-thĕuu mâi jer, hĕn yùu mêuua-gêe
ฉันหามือถือไม่เจอ เห็นอยู่เมื่อกี้
(can't find = hăa mâi jer [*cannot* exceptions, page 32])

Jane called a moment ago.
Jane thoo-maa mêuua-gêe
เจนโทรมาเมื่อกี้
(to call = thoo-hăa, call in = thoo-maa, call out = thoo-bpai)

just now

I **just** finished it.
phŏm **phêrng** tham sèd
ผมเพิ่งทำเสร็จ
(finished = sèd)

Peter just bought me this book.
Peter phêrng séuu năng-sĕuu lâem née hâi chăn
ปีเตอร์เพิ่งซื้อหนังสือเล่มนี้ให้ฉัน

I'm not hungry, I've just eaten.
chăn mâi hĭw, chăn phêrng gin
ฉันไม่หิว ฉันเพิ่งกิน

not long ago

We saw that movie **not long ago**.
rao duu năng rêuuang nán **mâi-naan-maa-née**
เราดูหนังเรื่องนั้นไม่นานมานี้

They moved to Bangkok not long ago.
phûuak-khăo yáai bpai grung-thâep mâi-naan-maa-née
พวกเขาย้ายไปกรุงเทพไม่นานมานี้
(move = yáai)

Peter got a new job not long ago.
Peter dâi ngaan mài mâi-naan-maa-née
ปีเตอร์ได้งานใหม่ไม่นานมานี้

recently

rew-rew-née is unusual in that it can mean *recently* in the past or *soon* in the near future.

If it's not understood from the context, use *mêuua* to be clear it's the past you're referring to, and use *jà* for the future. Compare these first two examples:

A new shopping mall opened **recently**.
mee hâang bpèrd mài **mêuua rew-rew-née**
มีห้างเปิดใหม่เมื่อเร็ว ๆ นี้

A new shopping mall will open **soon**.
jà mee hâang bpèrd mài **rew-rew-née**
จะมีห้างเปิดใหม่เร็ว ๆ นี้

I sold my car not long ago. I must buy a new one **soon**.
phŏm khăai ród bpai mâi-naan-maa-née, phŏm dtâwng séuu khan mài **rew-rew-née**
ผมขายรถไปไม่นานมานี้ ผมต้องซื้อคันใหม่เร็ว ๆ นี้

I've just been to see the doctor recently.
mêuua rew-rew-née, phŏm phêrng bpai hăa măw maa
เมื่อเร็ว ๆ นี้ ผมเพิ่งไปหาหมอมา

the other day

I had a lot of fun **the other day**. Can we meet again soon?
wan-gàwn chăn sà-nùk mâak, rao jà dâi phóp gan èek rew-rew-née măi?
วันก่อนฉันสนุกมาก เราจะได้พบกันอีกเร็ว ๆ นี้ไหม

We went to visit Jane in Hadyai the other day.
wan-gàwn rao bpai hăa Jane thêe hàad-yài
วันก่อนเราไปหาเจนที่หาดใหญ่

You already asked me that the other day.
khun thăam chăn láeo mêuua wan-gàwn
คุณถามฉันแล้วเมื่อวันก่อน

a long time ago, for a long time

The difference is understood from context.

She used to love me, but it was **a long time ago**.
ther khaey rák phŏm, dtàae man **naan-maa-láeo**
เธอเคยรักผม แต่มันนานมาแล้ว
(*khaey* tells us this is in the past)

The two of us have loved one another **for a long time**.
rao săwng khon rák gan **naan-maa-láeo**
เราสองคนรักกันนานมาแล้ว
(the sentence is in present tense)

in the past

"I heard he's dating Jane." "**In the past** yes, but not now."
"phŏm dâi-yin wâa khăo khóp gàp Jane" "**mêuua-gàwn** châi, dtàae mâi châi dtawn-née"
"ผมได้ยินว่าเขาคบกับเจน" "เมื่อก่อนใช่ แต่ไม่ใช่ตอนนี้"

I previously lived in England.
mêuua-gàwn chăn yùu thêe ang-grìd
เมื่อก่อนฉันอยู่ที่อังกฤษ

in the past

Chapter 32

Family relations

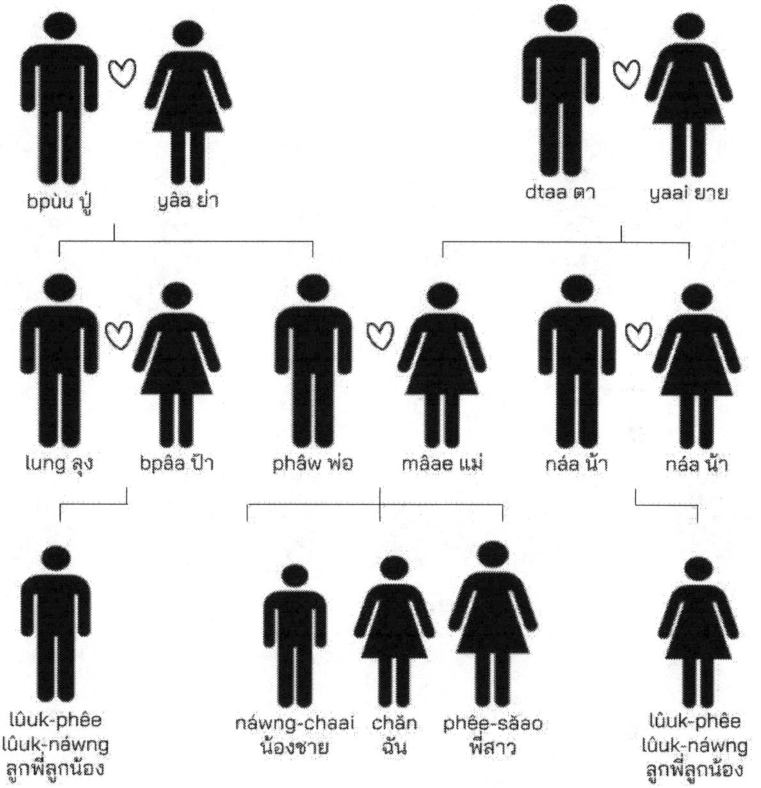

The words used for grandparents and parents-in-law differs for each parent's side of the family.

father's side	**mother's side**
grandfather bpùu ปู่	grandfather dtaa ตา
grandmother yâa ย่า	grandmother yaai ยาย

husband's father
phâw-săa-mee
พ่อสามี

husband's mother
mâae-săa-mee
แม่สามี

wife's father
phâw-dtaa
พ่อตา

wife's mother
mâae-yaai
แม่ยาย

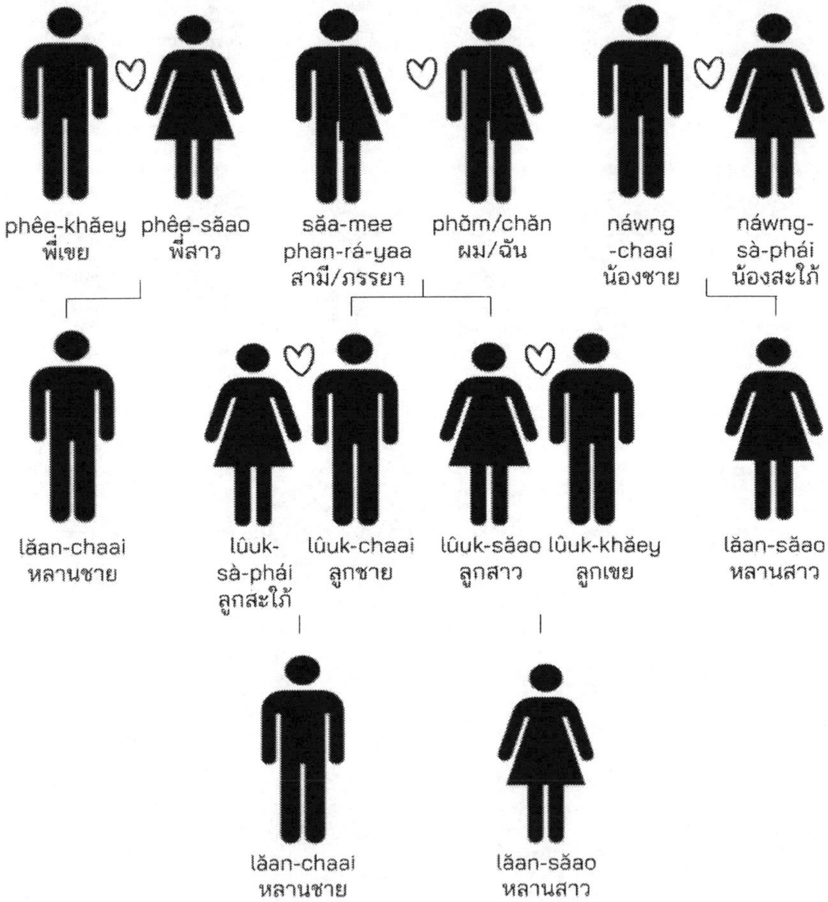

Summary of family members

father
phâw
พ่อ

mother
mâae
แม่

husband
săa-mee
สามี

wife
phan-rá-yaa/phan-yaa
ภรรยา

older brother
phêe-chaai
พี่ชาย

older sister
phêe-săao
พี่สาว

younger brother
náwng-chaai
น้องชาย

younger sister
náwng-săao
น้องสาว

uncle (older than parent)
lung
ลุง

aunt (older than parent)
bpâa
ป้า

uncle/aunt (younger than mother)
náa
น้า

uncle/aunt (younger than father)
aa
อา

son
lûuk-chaai
ลูกชาย

daughter
lûuk-săao
ลูกสาว

grandson/nephew
lăan-chaai
หลานชาย

granddaughter/niece
lăan-săao
หลานสาว

son-in-law
lûuk-khăey
ลูกเขย

daughter-in-law
lûuk-sà-phái
ลูกสะใภ้

older brother-in-law
phêe-khăey
พี่เขย

older sister-in-law
phêe-sà-phái
พี่สะใภ้

younger brother-in-law
náwng-khăey
น้องเขย

younger sister-in-law
náwng-sà-phái
น้องสะใภ้

cousins
lûuk-phêe lûuk-náwng
ลูกพี่ลูกน้อง

relatives
yâad
ญาติ

boy/girlfriend
faaen
แฟน

parents
phâw-mâae
พ่อแม่

family members

Appendix I

Most common classifiers

classifier	used for
lam ลำ	boats, ships, submarines, aeroplanes
sâen เส้น	hairs, threads, string, rope, noodles, spaghetti
phĕuun ผืน	towels, sheets, linen, mats, rugs, tablecloths
phàaen แผ่น	paper, CD, and thin or flat objects
lâem เล่ม	books, knives, scissors, candles
khùuad ขวด	bottles and bottled substances
thŭng ถุง	small bags (paper bags, shopping bags), pouches
glùm กลุ่ม	groups, bundles, clusters
grà-bpăwng กระป๋อง	tin cans, canned food and drink
méd เม็ด	small round items, e.g. buttons, tablets, sweets, seeds, beads, etc
dtuua ตัว	digits, numbers, and anything with limbs, e.g. bodies, shirts, trousers, suits, animals, fish, germs, chairs, tables, desks, etc.
gawng กอง	piles, heaps, military divisions
gâwn ก้อน	lumps, chunks, clouds, batteries, bar of soap or cheese or butter
baan บาน	doors, windows, mirrors, other glass panels

khâang ข้าง	sides
fawng ฟอง	eggs
khon คน	people
hâwng ห้อง	rooms
reuuan เรือน	watches and clocks
lûuk ลูก	round fruit, balls, round objects, storms
chà-bàp ฉบับ	periodicals, newspapers, documents, essays, letters, contracts
khan คัน	road vehicles, forks, umbrellas
chín ชิ้น	a piece of food, a piece of writing, a piece of work, any piece taken from a whole
an อัน	small things
hàaeng แห่ง	locations e.g. hotel
ngûuad งวด	instalment payments
bplaaeng แปลง	plots of land
rûup รูป	pictures, paintings, monks
dâam ด้าม	pens, brooms, brushes
jaan จาน	dishes, plates of food, satellite dishes

hŭua หัว	potatoes, head-like objects
yàang อย่าง	types, kinds, sorts, varieties, patterns
wong วง	rings, bracelets, circles, musical groups
săai สาย	roads, rivers, strings, wires
duuang ดวง	light bulbs, stamps, stars, medals
mái ไม้	wooden objects including sports racquets
roong โรง	buildings, structures
nâa หน้า	pages (a face of a page)
làwd หลอด	tube-like objects
méuu มื้อ	meals
rêuuang เรื่อง	stories, movies, dreams
hàw ห่อ	parcels, packages, wrapped items
khrêuuang เครื่อง	machinery
khráng ครั้ง	times, occasions
châw ช่อ	bunches, e.g. flowers, vegetables
gâaeo แก้ว	drinks served in a glass

chúd ชุด	collections or sets e.g. swimsuit, crockery, cutlery
fŭung ฝูง	herds or flocks
múuan ม้วน	rolls, e.g. film, sticky tape, bandages
dtà-làp ตลับ	small round cases or boxes
sêe ซี่	teeth, ribs, spokes, prongs, parallel items
khà-buuan ขบวน	trains, processions, convoys, parades
dtôn ต้น	trees, plants, posts, pillars, masts
phăaeng แผง	pills sold in plastic or foil sheets, screens
bai ใบ	bottles, glasses and other containers, leaves, sheets, leaflets, hats, bags, suitcases, the world, some fruits, playing cards, other flat objects or round, hollow items
thûuai ถ้วย	drinks served in a cup or mug
glàwng กล่อง	boxed items e.g. washing powder
lăng หลัง	houses, buildings, pianos
khûu คู่	pairs e.g. earrings, shoes
sawng ซอง	small packs or packages of things

common classifiers

Appendix II

Most common verbs

accept
yawm-ráp
ยอมรับ

agree
dtòk-long
ตกลง

allow
yawm-hâi / hâi
ยอมให้ /ให้

arrive
maa-thěung
มาถึง

ask
thăam
ถาม

ask for
khăw
ขอ

begin/start
rêrm
เริ่ม

believe
chêuua
เชื่อ

book
jawng
จอง

borrow
yeuum
ยืม

break
tham-sĭia
ทำเสีย

bring
nam-maa / phaa-maa
นำมา / พามา

brush
bpraaeng
แปรง

build
sâang
สร้าง

buy
séuu
ซื้อ

call
rîiak
เรียก

call (by phone)
thoo-hăa
โทรหา

can, be able
dâi
ได้

cancel
yók-lêrk
ยกเลิก

carry
thěuu
ถือ

catch
jàp
จับ

change
bplìian
เปลี่ยน

chat, talk
khui
คุย

choose
lêuuak
เลือก

clean
tham-khwaam-sà-àad
ทำความสะอาด

climb
bpeen
ปีน

close
bpìd
ปิด

come
maa
มา

contact
dtìd-dtàw
ติดต่อ

continue
dtàw
ต่อ

cook
tham-aa-hăan
ทำอาหาร

count
náp
นับ

crash
chon
ชน

cut
dtàd
ตัด

dance
dtâen
เต้น

decide
dtàd-sĭn
ตัดสิน

divorce
yàa
หย่า

do, make
tham
ทำ

draw
wâad
วาด

drink
dèuum
ดื่ม

drive
khàp
ขับ

eat
gin
กิน

end, finish
jòb
จบ

enjoy
sà-nùk
สนุก

explain
à-thí-baai
อธิบาย

fall
dtòk
ตก

feel
rúu-sèuk
รู้สึก

fight
sûu / dtàw-sûu
สู้ / ต่อสู้

fill
dterm
เติม

fill (in a form)
gràwk (bàaeb-fawm)
กรอก (แบบฟอร์ม)

find, look for
hăa
หา

finish
sèd
เสร็จ

fix, repair
sâwm
ซ่อม

flirt
jèeb
จีบ

fly
bin
บิน

follow
dtaam
ตาม

forget
leuum
ลืม

fry
thâwd
ทอด

give
hâi
ให้

go
bpai
ไป

go by, travel by
bpai-dooy
ไปโดย

happen
gèrd-khêun
เกิดขึ้น

have
mee
มี

have to, must
dtâwng
ต้อง

hear
dâi-yin
ได้ยิน

help
chûuai
ช่วย

hit
dtee
ตี

hope
wăng
หวัง

invite
chern / chuuan
เชิญ / ชวน

iron
rêed
รีด

keep
gèp
เก็บ

know
rúu
รู้

know (person/place)
rúu-jàk
รู้จัก

laugh
hŭua-ró
หัวเราะ

lead
nam
นำ

learn, study
riian
เรียน

leave
àwk bpai
ออกไป

let, allow
hâi
ให้

lie
goo-hòk
โกหก

lift
yók
ยก

like
châwp
ชอบ

listen
fang
ฟัง

look
duu
ดู

look after
duu-laae
ดูแล

lose, mislay
tham-hăai
ทำหาย

lose (not win)
pháae
แพ้

love
rák
รัก

marry
dtàaeng-ngaan
แต่งงาน

massage
nûuad
นวด

mean
mǎai-thěung
หมายถึง

meet
phóp
พบ

move
yáai
ย้าย

need
jam-bpen
จำเป็น

open
bpèrd
เปิด

order
sàng
สั่ง

organise, arrange
jàd
จัด

park a vehicle
jàwd
จอด

pass
phàan
ผ่าน

pay, spend
jàai
จ่าย

pick up, collect
ráp / gèp
รับ / เก็บ

play
lâen
เล่น

postpone
lêuuan
เลื่อน

press
gòd
กด

pronounce
àwk-sĭiang
ออกเสียง

pull
deung
ดึง

push
phlàk / dan
ผลัก / ดัน

put
sài
ใส่

reach, arrive
maa-thĕung / bpai-thĕung
มาถึง / ไปถึง

read
àan
อ่าน

receive
ráp
รับ

remember
jam
จำ

reply
dtàwb
ตอบ

rest
phák / yùd-phák
พัก, หยุดพัก

return
glàb
กลับ

ride
khèe
ขี่

run
wîng
วิ่ง

see
hĕn
เห็น

seem, appear
duu-mĕuuan / bpraa-gòd
ดูเหมือน / ปรากฏ

sell
khăai
ขาย

send
sòng
ส่ง

shake
khà-yào
เขย่า

shout
dtà-goon
ตะโกน

show
sà-daaeng
แสดง

shower
àap-nám
อาบน้ำ

sign (a signature)
sen
เซ็น

sing
ráwng-phlaeng
ร้องเพลง

sit
nâng
นั่ง

sleep
nawn
นอน

smile
yím
ยิ้ม

speak, talk, say
phûud
พูด

spell
sà-gòd
สะกด

stand
yeuun
ยืน

stay, live
phák-yùu / aa-săi-yùu
พักอยู่ / อาศัยอยู่

steal
khà-mooi
ขโมย

stop
yùd
หยุด

support
sà-nàp-sà-nŭn
สนับสนุน

sweep
gwàad
กวาด

swim
wâai-nám
ว่ายน้ำ

take
phaa-bpai / ao-bpai
พาไป / เอาไป

teach
sǎwn
สอน

tell
bàwk
บอก

think
khíd
คิด

throw away
thíng
ทิ้ง

tie
phùuk
ผูก

translate
bplaae
แปล

travel
thîiao
เที่ยว

try
lawng
ลอง

turn off
bpìd
ปิด

turn on
bpèrd
เปิด

type
phim
พิมพ์

understand
khâo-jai
เข้าใจ

use
chái
ใช้

wait
raw
รอ

wake up
dtèuun
ตื่น

walk
dern
เดิน

want to
dtâwng-gaan
ต้องการ

wash (general)
láang
ล้าง

watch
duu
ดู

win
chá-ná
ชนะ

wipe
chéd
เช็ด

work
tham-ngaan
ทำงาน

would like to
yàak-jà
อยากจะ

worry
gang-won
กังวล

write
khǐian
เขียน

Appendix III

Most common nouns

For places, see chapter 8 and appendix VI.

For parts of the day see chapters 13 & 16.

For family members see chapter 32.

air-con
aae
แอร์

alley
soy
ซอย

animals
sàd
สัตว์

apple
áaep-bpêrn
แอปเปิ้ล

back
dâan-lăng
ด้านหลัง

beach
hàad
หาด

bed
dtiiang
เตียง

belly, stomach
tháwng
ท้อง

bird
nók
นก

body hair
khŏn
ขน

book
năng-sĕuu
หนังสือ

bottle
khùuad
ขวด

box
glàwng
กล่อง

breeze, wind
lom
ลม

bridge, pier
sà-phaan
สะพาน

building, structure
dtèuk
ตึก

canal
khlawng
คลอง

cat
maaeo
แมว

ceremony
phí-thee
พิธี

chair
gâo-êe
เก้าอี้

chapter, lesson
bòd
บท

chicken
gài
ไก่

child
dèk
เด็ก

cloth, fabric
phâa
ผ้า

cloud
mâek
เมฆ

colour, paint
sĕe
สี

computer
khawm-piw-dtêr
คอมพิวเตอร์

contract
săn-yaa
สัญญา

country
bprà-thâed
ประเทศ

cow
wuua
วัว

cup
thûuai
ถ้วย

cupboard, cabinet
dtûu
ตู้

debt
nêe
หนี้

denim jeans
gaang-gaeng-yeen
กางเกงยีนส์

disease
rôok
โรค

district
am-pher
อำเภอ

document
àek-gà-săan
เอกสาร

dog
măa
หมา

door
bprà-dtuu
ประตู

ear(s)
hŭu
หู

egg
khài
ไข่

errand
thú-rá
ธุระ

eye
dtaa
ตา

face
nâa
หน้า

family
khrâwb-khruua
ครอบครัว

fan
phád-lom
พัดลม

fat
man
มัน

fever
khâi
ไข้

field, park
sà-năam
สนาม

finger, toe
níu
นิ้ว

fire
fai
ไฟ

firm, company
baw-rí-sàd
บริษัท

first name
chêuu
ชื่อ

fish
bplaa
ปลา

flag
thong
ธง

floor
phéuun
พื้น

flowers
dàwk-mái
ดอกไม้

food
aa-hăan
อาหาร

foot, feet
tháo
เท้า

foreigner
fà-ràng
ฝรั่ง

fork
sâwm
ส้อม

fridge
dtûu-yen
ตู้เย็น

friend
phêuuan
เพื่อน

front
dâan-nâa
ด้านหน้า

fruit
phŏn-lá-mái
ผลไม้

garden
sŭuan
สวน

ghost
phĕe
ผี

glass
gâaeo
แก้ว

gold
thawng
ทอง

guard, watchman
yaam
ยาม

guest
khàaek
แขก

hair (of the head)
phŏm
ผม

half
khrêung
ครึ่ง

hand(s)
meuu
มือ

handbag
grà-bpăo
กระเป๋า

hat
mùuak
หมวก

head
hŭua
หัว

health
sùk-khà-phâap
สุขภาพ

hill
nern-khăo
เนินเขา

hole
ruu
รู

horse
máa
ม้า

house, home
bâan
บ้าน

idea
khwaam-khíd
ความคิด

information
khâw-muun
ข้อมูล

insect
má-laaeng
แมลง

island
gò
เกาะ

junction, intersection
yâaek
แยก

kettle
gaa-dtôm-nám-ráwn
กาต้มน้ำร้อน

knife
mêed
มีด

lamp
khoom-fai
โคมไฟ

language
phaa-săa
ภาษา

lawsuit
khá-dee
คดี

left
sáai
ซ้าย

leg
khâa
ขา

letter
jòd-mǎai
จดหมาย

level, rank
chán
ชั้น

lid, cover
fǎa
ฝา

luck
chôok
โชค

machine
khrêuuang
เครื่อง

man
phûu-chaai
ผู้ชาย

marina, dock, wharf
thâa-reuua
ท่าเรือ

market
dtà-làad
ตลาด

meat
néuua
เนื้อ

medicine, drugs
yaa
ยา

microwave
mai-khroo-wâeb
ไมโครเวฟ

milk
nom
นม

money, silver
ngern
เงิน

monk, priest
phrá
พระ

monkey
ling
ลิง

mosquito
yung
ยุง

mountain
phuu-khǎo
ภูเขา

mouse, rat
nǔu
หนู

mouth
bpàak
ปาก

neck
khaw
คอ

news
khàao
ข่าว

newspaper
nǎng-sěuu-phim
หนังสือพิมพ์

normal
tham-má-daa
ธรรมดา

notebook
nóed-búk
โน๊ตบุ๊ค

notepad
sà-mùd
สมุด

number
ber
เบอร์

occasion,opportunity
oo-gàad
โอกาส

oil, fuel
nám-man
น้ำมัน

orange
sôm
ส้ม

paper
grà-dàad
กระดาษ

pen
bpàak-gaa
ปากกา

pencil
din-sǎw
ดินสอ

person, people
khon
คน

picture, drawing
phâap
ภาพ

pig, pork
mŭu
หมู

pipe
thâw
ท่อ

plate
jaan
จาน

plot of land
bplaaeng
แปลง

position, post
dtam-nàaeng
ตำแหน่ง

price
raa-khaa
ราคา

problem
bpan-hăa
ปัญหา

product
sĭn-kháa
สินค้า

profit
gam-rai
กำไร

province
jang-wàd
จังหวัด

quantity
jam-nuuan
จำนวน

question
kham-thăam
คำถาม

queue, a row
thăaew
แถว

rai - land measure
râi
ไร่

rain
fŏn
ฝน

reason
hàed-phŏn
เหตุผล

religion
sàad-sà-năa
ศาสนา

remote control
ree-mòed
รีโมท

right
khwăa
ขวา

river
mâae-nám
แม่น้ำ

road
thà-nŏn
ถนน

room
hâwng
ห้อง

sea
thá-lae
ทะเล

sentence
bprà-yàok
ประโยค

service
baw-rí-gaan
บริการ

shirt/blouse
sêuua
เสื้อ

shoes
rawng-tháo
รองเท้า

shop
ráan
ร้าน

shorts
gaang-gaeng-khăa-sân
กางเกงขาสั้น

size
khà-nàad
ขนาด

skirt
grà-bproong
กระโปรง

sky
fáa
ฟ้า

smartphone
meuu-thĕuu
มือถือ

snake
nguu
งู

sofa
soo-faa
โซฟา

soil, dirt
din
ดิน

soldier
thá-hăan
ทหาร

sound
sĭiang
เสียง

spoon
cháwn
ช้อน

stairs
ban-dai
บันได

station
sà-thăa-nee
สถานี

student
nák-riian
นักเรียน

sub-district
dtam-bon
ตำบล

suitcase
grà-bpăo-dern-thaang
กระเป๋าเดินทาง

sunshine
dàaed
แดด

swimming pool
sà-wâai-nám
สระว่ายน้ำ

T-shirt
sêuua-yêuud
เสื้อยืด

table
dtóe
โต๊ะ

tablet
tháaeb-lèd
แท็บเล็ต

tax
phaa-sĕe
ภาษี

tea
chaa
ชา

temple
wád
วัด

ticket
dtŭua
ตั๋ว

time
waeh-laa
เวลา

times, occasions
khráng
ครั้ง

tongue
lín
ลิ้น

tooth
fan
ฟัน

top, peak
yâwd
ยอด

town
meuuang
เมือง

truth
khwaam-jing
ความจริง

TV
thee-wee
ทีวี

umbrella
rôm
ร่ม

vehicle
ród
รถ

wardrobe
dtûu-sêuua-phâa
ตู้เสื้อผ้า

watch, clock
naa-lí-gaa
นาฬิกา

water
nám
น้ำ

way, method
wí-thee
วิธี

window
nâa-dtàang
หน้าต่าง

woman
phûu-yĭng
ผู้หญิง

woods, forest
bpàa
ป่า

word
kham
คำ

work, job
ngaan
งาน

world
lôok
โลก

Appendix IV

Most common adjectives

angry
gròod
โกรธ

annoying
nâa-ram-khaan
น่ารำคาญ

bad
mâi-dee
ไม่ดี

beautiful
sŭuai
สวย

big
yài
ใหญ่

busy
yûng
ยุ่ง

calm, peaceful
sà-ngòp
สงบ

cheap
thùuk
ถูก

clean
sà-àad
สะอาด

clever
chà-làad
ฉลาด

closed
bpìd
ปิด

cold
yen
เย็น

delicious
à-ròy
อร่อย

difficult
yâak
ยาก

dirty
sòk-gà-bpròk
สกปรก

easy
ngâai
ง่าย

empty
bplào
เปล่า

expensive
phaaeng
แพง

famous
mee-chêuu-sĭiang
มีชื่อเสียง

far
glai
ไกล

forceful, strong
raaeng
แรง

full
dtem
เต็ม

fun
sà-nùk
สนุก

funny
dtà-lòk
ตลก

good
dee
ดี

hard (firm)
khăeng
แข็ง

healthy
mee-sùk-khà-phâap-dee
มีสุขภาพดี

heavy
nàk
หนัก

high
sŭung
สูง

honest
sêuu-sàd
ซื่อสัตย์

hot
ráwn
ร้อน

humid
chéuun
ชื้น

interesting
nâa-sǒn-jai
น่าสนใจ

kind
jai-dee
ใจดี

light
bao
เบา

lonely
ngǎo
เหงา

long
yaao
ยาว

low
dtàm
ต่ำ

low (height)
dtîia
เตี้ย

narrow
khâaep
แคบ

near
glâi
ใกล้

new
mài
ใหม่

old (objects)
gào
เก่า

old (people)
gàae
แก่

open
bpèrd
เปิด

polite
sù-phâap
สุภาพ

poor
yâak-jon
ยากจน

proud
phuum-jai
ภูมิใจ

rich
ruuai
รวย

sad
sâo
เศร้า

scary
nâa-gluua
น่ากลัว

sharp (pointed)
lǎaem
แหลม

sharp (blade)
khom
คม

short
sân
สั้น

sick, unwell
bpùuai
ป่วย

small
lék
เล็ก

soft
nûm
นุ่ม

strong
khǎeng-raaeng
แข็งแรง

tall
sǔung
สูง

tired
nèùuai
เหนื่อย

ugly
nâa-glìiad
น่าเกลียด

warm
ùn
อุ่น

wide
gwâang
กว้าง

Appendix V

Jobs & professions

accountant
nák-ban-chee
นักบัญชี

actor
nák-sà-daaeng
นักแสดง

agent
dtuua-thaaen
ตัวแทน

architect
sà-thăa-bpà-ník
สถาปนิก

baker
khon-tham-khà-nŏm-bpang
คนทำขนมปัง

barber
châang-tham-phŏm/châang-dtàd-phŏm
ช่างทำผม/ช่างตัดผม

boss
hŭua-nâa
หัวหน้า

bricklayer
châang-bpuun
ช่างปูน

builder
châang-gàw-sâang
ช่างก่อสร้าง

carpenter
châang-mái
ช่างไม้

cashier
kháaed-chiia
แคชเชียร์

chef
phâw-khruua
พ่อครัว

chemist
phae-sàd-chá-gawn
เภสัชกร

cook
mâae-khruua
แม่ครัว

dentist
than-dtà-phâaed/măw-fan
ทันตแพทย์/หมอฟัน

doctor
măw
หมอ

draftsman
châang-khĭian-bàaeb
ช่างเขียนแบบ

driver
khon-khàp-ród
คนขับรถ

electrician
châang-fai-fáa
ช่างไฟฟ้า

employee
phá-nák-ngaan
พนักงาน/ลูกจ้าง

engineer
wíd-sà-wá-gawn
วิศวกร

farmer
chaao-naa
ชาวนา

fireman
phá-nák-ngaan-dàp-phlerng
พนักงานดับเพลิง

fisherman
chaao-bprà-mong
ชาวประมง

gardener
khon-sŭuan
คนสวน

hairdresser
châang-tham-phŏm
ช่างทำผม

journalist
nák-khàao
นักข่าว

labourer
khon-ngaan/gam-má-gawn
คนงาน/กรรมกร

lawyer
thá-naai-khwaam
ทนายความ

maid
mâae-bâan
แม่บ้าน

manager
phûu-jàd-gaan
ผู้จัดการ

mechanic
châang-khrêuuang
ช่างเครื่อง

nurse
phá-yaa-baan
พยาบาล

pharmacist
phae-sàd-chá-gawn
เภสัชกร

photographer
châang-phâap
ช่างภาพ

pilot
nák-bin
นักบิน

plumber
châang-bprà-bpaa
ช่างประปา

policeman
dtam-rùuad
ตำรวจ

politician
nák-gaan-meuuang
นักการเมือง

postman
bù-rùd-bprai-sà-nee
บุรุษไปรษณีย์

professor
aa-jaan
อาจารย์

real estate agent
naai-nâa
นายหน้า

retired
gà-sĭian
เกษียณ

secretary
lae-khăa
เลขา

steelworker
châang-lèk
ช่างเหล็ก

student
nák-riian
นักเรียน

tailor
châang-dtàd-sêuua
ช่างตัดเสื้อ

teacher
khruu
ครู

unemployed
wâang-ngaan
ว่างงาน

vet
sàd-dtà-wá-phâaed
สัตวแพทย์

waiter/waitress
phá-nák-ngaan-sèrp
พนักงานเสิร์ฟ

worker
khon-ngaan
คนงาน

Appendix VI

Places

airport
sà-năam-bin
สนามบิน

amusement park
sŭuan-sà-nùk
สวนสนุก

bakery
bae-ger-rêe
เบเกอรี่

bank
thá-naa-khaan
ธนาคาร

barber's shop
ráan-dtàd-phŏm
ร้านตัดผม

bathroom
hâwng-nám
ห้องน้ำ

beauty salon
ráan-sĕrm-sŭuai
ร้านเสริมสวย

bedroom
hâwng-nawn
ห้องนอน

bookshop
ráan-năng-sĕuu
ร้านหนังสือ

building supplies store
ráan-wád-sà-dù-gàw-sâang
ร้านวัสดุก่อสร้าง

bus station
sà-thăa-nee-khŏn-sòng
สถานีรถขนส่ง

cafe
khaa-fâe
คาเฟ่

car park
laan-jàwd-ród
ลานจอดรถ

car repair workshop
ùu-sâwm-ród
อู่ซ่อมรถ

chemist/pharmacy
ráan-khăai-yaa
ร้านขายยา

cinema
roong-năng
โรงหนัง

clothes shop
ráan-sêuua-phâa
ร้านเสื้อผ้า

coffee shop
ráan-gaa-faae
ร้านกาแฟ

district office
am-pher
อำเภอ

embassy
sà-thăan-thûud
สถานทูต

factory
roong-ngaan
โรงงาน

gym
yim
ยิม

hospital
roong-phá-yaa-baan
โรงพยาบาล

hotel
roong-raaem
โรงแรม

house, home
bâan
บ้าน

jewellery shop
ráan-khăai-khrêuuang-bprà-dàb
ร้านขายเครื่องประดับ

kitchen
khruua
ครัว

language school
roong-riian-săwn-phaa-săa
โรงเรียนสอนภาษา

laundromat
ráan-sák-rêed
ร้านซักรีด

library
hâwng-sà-mùd
ห้องสมุด

living room
hâwng-nâng-lâen
ห้องนั่งเล่น

market
dtà-làad
ตลาด

municipal office
thâed-sà-baan
เทศบาล

museum
phí-phíd-thá-phan
พิพิธภัณฑ์

office
săm-nák-ngaan
สำนักงาน

petrol/gas station
bpám-nám-man
ปั๊มน้ำมัน

police station
sà-thăa-nee dtam-rùuad
สถานีตำรวจ

post office
bprai-sà-nee
ไปรษณีย์

public park
sŭuan-săa-thaa-rá-ná
สวนสาธารณะ

railway station
sà-thăa-nee ród-fai
สถานีรถไฟ

restaurant
ráan-aa-hăan
ร้านอาหาร

school
roong-riian
โรงเรียน

shoe shop
ráan-rawng-tháo
ร้านรองเท้า

shop
ráan
ร้าน

shopping mall
hâang-sàp-phá-sĭn-kháa
ห้างสรรพสินค้า

stationery shop
ráan-khrêuuang-khĭian
ร้านเครื่องเขียน

store room
hâwng-gèp-khăwng
ห้องเก็บของ

supermarket
suu-bpêr-maa-géd
ซูเปอร์มาร์เก็ต

temple
wád
วัด

town hall
săa-laa-glaang
ศาลากลาง

toy shop
ráan-khăai-khăwng-lâen
ร้านขายของเล่น

university
má-hăa-wíd-thá-yaa-lai
มหาวิทยาลัย

village
mùu-bâan
หมู่บ้าน

zoo
sŭuan-sàd
สวนสัตว์

Appendix VII

Months of the year

January
mók-gà-raa-khom
มกราคม

February
gum-phaa-phan
กุมภาพันธ์

March
mee-naa-khom
มีนาคม

April
maeh-săa-yon
เมษายน

May
phréud-sà-phaa-khom
พฤษภาคม

June
mí-thù-naa-yon
มิถุนายน

July
gà-rá-gà-daa-khom
กรกฎาคม

August
sĭng-hăa-khom
สิงหาคม

September
gan-yaa-yon
กันยายน

October
dtù-laa-khom
ตุลาคม

November
phréud-sà-jì-gaa-yon
พฤศจิกายน

December
than-waa-khom
ธันวาคม

The ending syllables of the words tell us how many days there are in each month.

Months with 30 days end with -yon.

Months with 31 days end with -khom.

Of course, only Feburary ends with -phan.

The year in Thailand is very often shown using the Buddhist year, which is 543 years ahead of the Gregorian system. Just add or subtract either way to calculate one or the other.

months of the year

A

àad (jà), 151
aae, 38
áaep-bpêrn, 58
aa-hăan, 37
aa-hăan-cháo, 76
aa-hăan glaang-wan, 76
aa-hăan-wâang, 76
aa-hăan-yen, 76
àan, 14
aa-thíd, 73
àek-gà-săan, 58
am-pher, 47
an, 57
ang-grìd, 29
ao, 63
à-rai, 78
à-ròy, 105
àwk, 33, 118
àwk-gam-lang-gaai, 146

B

baa, 47
bàai, 85
bâan, 47, 58
baang, 111, 145
bâang, 110
baang khráng, 148
bai, 57
bao, 39
bàwk, 82
bin, 19
bon, 116
bòy, 144
bpàaed, 7
bpai, 14
bpai-thĕung, 121
bpee, 74
bpee-nâa, 74
bpee-née, 74
bpee-thêe-láeo, 74
bpen, 43
bpèrd, 38
bpìd, 38
bplào, 39
bpòk-gà-dtì, 149
bprà-dtuu, 38
bprà-jam, 144
bprai-sà-nee, 47
bprà-thâed, 93
bpuu, 146
bùuak, 11

C

chaa, 69
chà-bàp, 57
chái, 92
châi măi, 54
chăn, 13

cháo, 85
cháwn, 37
châwp, 16
chee-wíd, 149
chín, 56
chûua-moong, 85

D

dâi, 29
dâi-yin, 16
dee, 105
dee-gwàa, 114
dern, 19
deuuan, 73
deuuan-nâa, 74
deuuan-née, 74
deuuan-thêe-láeo, 74
dèuum, 14
diaao, 65
diaao-gan, 103
dtàae, 83
dtàaek-dtàang, 104
dtàang, 104
dtâi, 116
dtà-làad, 47
dtà-làwd, 148
dtâng-dtàae, 119
dtawn, 85, 119
dtawn-bàai, 75
dtawn-cháo, 75
dtawn-glaang-kheuun, 75
dtawn-khâm, 75
dtawn-née, 74
dtawn-yen, 75
dtâwng, 112
dtâwng-gaan, 17
dtee, 85
dtem, 39
dtîia, 39
dtóe, 37
dtòk, 80
dtrong, 85
dtrong-glaang, 118
dtrong-khâam, 116
dtuua, 56
dtǔua, 58
dtûu-sêuua-phâa, 37
dtûu-yen, 37
duu, 14
dûuai, 133
dûuai-gan, 133

E

-èd, 8
èek, 74

F

fang, 16
fǒn, 80

G

gàae, 39
gâaeo, 37
gaa-dtôm-nám-ráwn, 37
gaa-faae, 47
gaan-, 138, 141-142
gaang-gaeng-khăa-sân, 38
gaang-gaeng-yeen, 37
gài, 70
gâo, 7
gào, 39
gâo-êe, 37
gàp, 22
gâw, 127
gàwn, 114, 119
gèe, 71
gern-bpai, 107
gì-loo, 69
gin, 14
glaang-wan, 75
glàb, 114
glàb-bâan, 114
glâi, 105
glai, 105
grà-bpăo, 38
grà-bproong, 38
grà-dàad, 58
grung-thâep, 20
gwàa, 105
gwâang, 39

H

hâa, 7
hăan, 11
hâang, 117
hâang-sàp-phá-sĭn-kháa, 117
hâi, 129
hâi gàp, 129
hâwng, 57
hâwng-nám, 93
hĕn, 16
hòk, 7
hŭua-nâa, 114

J

jà, 24
jàak, 104, 118
jàak ... thĕung ..., 119
jaan, 37
jai-, -jai, 153
jam, 16
jam-bpen-dtâwng, 113
jang-see-lawn, 47
jàwd, 117
jèd, 7
jer, 92
jòd-măai, 58
(jon) thĕung, 119
jùd, 7

K

khâ, 12
khâaep, 39
khăai, 48
khâao, 69
khaey, 144
khăo, 13
khâo, 118
khâo-jai, 16
khan, 56
khâang-bâan, 118
khâang-bon, 118
khâang-khâang, 116
khâang-lâang, 118
khâang-lăng, 116
khâang-nâa, 116
khâang-nai, 116
khâang-nâwk, 116
khàp, 19
khăw, 136
khăw hâi, 136
khawm-piw-dtêr, 38
khăwng, 43, 124
khăwng-chăn, 43
khăwng-khăo, 43
khăwng-khrai, 45
khăwng-khun, 43
khăwng-man, 43
khăwng-phŏm, 43
khăwng-phûuak-khăo, 43
khăwng-phûuak-rao, 43
khăwng-ther, 43
khèe, 19
khèed, 69
kheuu, 51
kheuun-née, 75
khíd, 14
khĭian, 14
khom, 39
khon, 57
khrai, 45
khráng, 57
khráp, 12
khrêung, 69, 85
khrêuuang, 57
khruua, 118
khui, 92
khun, 13
khùuad, 57
khuuan (jà), 114
khuun, 11
khwaam-, 138-140

L

lá, 147
lăaem, 39
lăai, 65
láan, 9
laan-jàwd-ród, 117

láe, 24
lâem, 57
láeo, 95, 128
láeo-gâw, 135
lăng, 57, 119
lăng (jàak), 119
làp, 33
lék, 38
líd, 69
lób, 11
lûuk, 57

M

maa, 14
măa, 58
mâae-bâan, 118
maaeo, 58
mâak, 107
mâak gwàa, 109
mâak thêe-sùd, 109
mài, 39
măi, 26
mâi, 21
mái, 135
mâi-dâi, 30
mâi gèe, 65
mai-khroo-wâeb, 37
mâi-naan-maa-née, 158
mák-jà, 148
man, 13
mawng, 33
maw-ther-sai, 19
mee, 60
mêed, 37
meuu, 133
mêuua, 119
mêuua-gàwn, 158
mêuua-gêe, 158
mĕuuan, 102
mĕuuan-gan, 102
mêuua-rài, 78
mêuua-waan-née, 74
mêuua-waan-seuun, 74
mèuun, 9
meuu-thĕuu, 38
moong, 85
mŭu, 70
mùuak, 38
mùu-bâan, 47

N

nâa, 75
nâa-, 155
nâa-dtàang, 38
nâa-jà, 114
naan-maa-láeo, 158
nâa-sŏn-jai, 106
naa-thee, 85
năi, 92
nai, 102, 116

nàk, 39
nárn, 37
nám-áaep-bpêrn, 70
nám-dtaan, 70
nám-man-phêuud, 70
nám-sôm, 70
nân, 43
nán, 62
nâng, 14
năng, 134
năng-sĕuu, 58
năng-sĕuu-phim, 58
nâwk-jàak, 125
nawn, 14
nêe, 43
née, 62
néuk, 82
nèung, 7
néuua, 70
nĕuua, 116
nèuuai, 14
ngâai, 105
ngaan, 82
nóed-búk, 38
nom, 70
nòy, 136
nóy, 106, 110, 153

P

phaaeng, 105
phaai-nai, 74
phaa-săa, 29
phád-lom, 38
phan, 9
phêrng, 158
phêuuan, 57
phìd, 139, 150
phŏm, 13
phóp, 92
phró (wâa), 151
phrûng-née, 74
phûuak-khăo, 13
phûuak-rao, 13
phûu-chaai, 58
phûu-yĭng, 58
phûud, 14

R

raa-khaa, 36, 66, 68
ráan, 47
ráan-aa-hăan, 47
ráan-gaa-faae, 47
ráan khăai khà-nŏm-bpang, 117
rák, 16
raa-dtree-sà-wàd, 35
ráp, 135
raw, 16
rá-wàang, 116
ráwn, 39, 106

ree-mòed, 38
rĕuu, 99, 101
rêuuai-rêuuai, 148
rêuuang, 156
rew-rew-née, 158
riian, 92
ród-fai, 19
ród-yon, 19
ród-maw-ther-sai, 19
rôm, 38
roong-năng, 47
roong-phá-yaa-baan, 48
roong-raaem, 47
roong-riian, 47
róy, 9
rúu, 14
rúu-jàk, 16

S

sà-àad, 39
săaen, 9
săam, 7
săa-mee, 146
sà-baai, 35
sae-wên, 47
sà-mĕr, 148
sân, 39
sà-năam-bin, 47
sà-nùk, 106
săn-yaa, 58
sâo, 131
sà-wàd-dee, 35
sâwm, 37
săwng, 7
sà-thăa-nee dtam-rùuad, 48
sà-thăa-nee ród-fai, 48
sà-thăan-thûud, 47
sèd, 158
sèe, 7
sĕe, 40
sĕe-daaeng, 40
sĕe-dam, 40
sĕe-fáa, 40
sĕe-khăao, 40
sĕe-khĭaao, 40
sĕe-lĕuuang, 40
sĕe-nám-ngern, 40
sĕe-thao, 40
sen-thrân, 47
séuu, 48
séuu-khăwng, 92
sêuua, 37
sêuua-yêuud, 37
sĭia-jai, 35
sìp, 7
sòk-gà-bpròk, 39
soo-faa, 37
sôm, 58
sŭuai, 105

sŭun, 7
sŭung, 39

T

thâa, 115, 127
thaan, 76
tham, 14
tham-dûuai, 133
tham-hâi, 131
tham-mai, 79
tham-ngaan, 14
thá-naa-khaan, 47
thâo-gàp, 11
thâo-rài, 85
tháp, 10
tháaeb-lèd, 38
thêe, 47, 92
thêe-láeo, 74
thêe-năi, 49
thêe-nân, 18
thêe-nâng, 114
thêe-nêe, 18
thêe-sùd, 105
thee-wee, 38
ther, 13
thĕung, 119
thîaao, 147
thîiang-kheuun, 85
thîiang-wan, 85
thoo-hăa, 16, 158
thúk, 123
thûm, 85
thûuai, 37
thùuk, 105

U

ùn, 39

W

wâa, 80
wâai-nám, 14
wàd, 36
waeh-laa, 85
wan, 73
wan-aa-thíd, 12
wan-ang-khaan, 12
wan-gàwn, 158
wan-née, 74
wan-jan, 73
wan-má-reuun-née, 74
wan-phá-réu-hàd, 12
wan-phúd, 12
wan-săo, 12
wan-sùk, 12
wí-naa-thee, 85
wîng, 19

Y

yáai, 159
yâak, 105
yàak dâi, 63

yàak (jà), 17

yàang-rai, 79

yaao, 39

yài, 38

yang, 99

yêe-sìp, 8

yen, 39, 85

yér, 110

yin-dee, 35

yók-wáen, 124

yûng, 36

yùu, 47

A

ability
  can, 29
  cannot, 30
  can ...?, 31
  exceptions, 32
above, 116
across, 116
adjectives, 40
adjectives as verbs, 41
after, 119
afternoon
  early afternoon, 75, 85
  late afternoon, 75, 85
  this afternoon, 76
ago, 74
air-con, 38
airport, 47
a little, 106, 110, 153
allow, 129
alone, 65
a lot, 65, 110
alphabet, 3-5
also, 133
always, 148
am, is, are, 43, 47, 51
and, 24
and then, 135
answering questions, 27, 54
apple, 58
apple juice, 70
asking questions, 26
at, 47, 85

B

bank, 47
bar, 47
because, 151
beef, 70
been, 98
before, 119
behind, 116
below, 116
beside, 116
besides, 125
better, 114
between, 116
big, 38
black, 40
blade, 39
blouse, 37
blue, 40
bold, 153
book, 58
bottle, 57
brave, 153
breakfast, 76
broadminded, 153
but, 83
buy, 48
by, 133

C

call (by phone), 16
calm, 153
can, 29
can questions, 31
cannot, 30

cannot exceptions, 33
cat, 58
cause, 129
chair, 37
chat, 92
chicken, 70
cinema, 47
classifiers, 56, 164-167
clean, 39
closed, 38
coffee shop, 47
cold, 39
colour, 40
come, 14
comparisons, 102-109
computer, 38
conditional clauses, 127-128
conjunctions
  also, 133
  and 24
  and then, 135
  but, 83
  that, as, 80
  too, 133
  with, 22
contract, 58
cost, 36, 66, 68
cup, 37

D

day, 73
  the other day, 158
days of the week, 12
decimal point, 7
denim jeans, 37
different, 104
dinner, 76
dirty, 39
district office, 47
divide, 11
drive, 19
do, 14
document, 58
dog, 58
do not, does not, 21
door, 38
drink, 14
downstairs, 118
during, 119

E

each, 123
eat, 14
embassy, 47
empty, 39
ending consonants, 4
enter, 118
equals, 11
evening, 75, 85
  this evening, 76
ever, 144
every, 123
exactly, 85
except, 124
exit, 118

F

family, 161
fan, 38
few, 65, 110

fly, 19
Friday, 12
food, 37
for, 129
fork, 37
frequency, 144-150
fridge, 37
friend, 57
from, 104
from ... to ..., 119
full, 39
future tense, 24, 95

G

generous, 153
a glass, 37
give, 129
glad, 153
go, 14
  go in, 118
  go out, 118
gone, 98
goodbye, 35
goodnight, 35
green, 40
greetings, 35
grey, 40

H

half, 69
handbag, 38
happy, 153, 154
has, 60
hat, 38
have, 60
have to, 112
he, 13
hear, 16
heavy (weight), 39
hello, 35
her, 13
hers, 43
here, 18
high, 39
him, 13
his, 43
home, 47
hospital, 48
hot, 39
hot-headed, 153
hotel, 47
hour, 85
house, 47
how, 79
how many, 71

I

I, 13
if, 127
in, inside, 116
in front of, 116
initial consonants, 3
is, am, are, 43, 47, 51
is at, 47
it, 13
its, 43

J

jeans, 37
just now, 158

K

kettle, 37
kilogram, 69
kind, 153
kitchen, 118
knife, 37
know (a fact), 14
know (a person), 16

L

laptop computer, 38
large, 38
leave, 118
letter, 58
life, 149
light (weight), 39
like, 16
listen, 16
litre, 69
little, 106, 110, 153
long, 39
look, 14
love, 16
low, 39
lunch, 76

M

made of, made from, 133
make, 14
man, men, 58
many, 65
market, 47
maybe, 151
me, 13
mealtimes, 76
meet, 92
microwave, 37
midday, 75
in the middle, 118
midnight, 85
might, 151
milk, 70
mine, 43
minus, 11
a minute, 85
mobile phone, 38
a moment ago, 158
Monday, 11
month, 73
  this month, 74
  next month, 74
  last month, 74
more, 74
more -er, 105
morning, 75, 85
  this morning, 76
most -est, 105
motivation, 154
much, 110
multiply, 11
must 112
my, 43

N

narrow, 39
narrow-minded, 153
nasty, 153
necessary, 113
need to, 112
negatives, 21

negative verb-to-be, 51
never, 144
new, 39
newspaper, 58
next, 74
next door, 118
next to, 116
night, 75
no, not, 21
noon, 75
normally, 149
notebook computer, 38
not many, 67
not much, 110
not yet, 99
now, 74
numbers, 7-10

O

o'clock, 85
off, 38
often, 144
old, 39
on, 38, 116
open, 38
opposite, 116
or, 101
orange, 58
orange juice, 70
ought to, 114
our/ours, 43
outside, 116

P

paper, 58
parts of the day, 75
past tense, 95-101, 158-160
perhaps, 151
person, people, 57
personal pronouns, 13
phonetic alphabet, 3-5
plate, 37
pleased, 154
plus, 11
pointed, 39
points in time, 73
police station, 48
polite particles, 12
pork, 70
possibly, 151
possessive adjectives, 43
possessive pronouns, 44
post office, 47
prefixes, 138-143, 153
prepositions of place, 117-119
prepositions of time
  after, 121
  before, 120
  from ... to ..., 120
  since, 119
  until 120
  when, 121
  while, whilst, during, 121
price, 36, 66, 68
pronouns, 13
proud, 154

Q

quantifiers, 65
  a lot, 110

few, a little, 110
many, 66
much, 110
not a little, 110
not a lot, 110
not many, 67
only one, 68
some, 110
very few, very little, 110
questions, 26
question tags, 53
question words, 78

R

railway station, 48
rarely, 148
read, 14
receive, 135
recently, 158
red, 40
refrigerator, 37
regularly, 144
relative pronoun, 93
relatives, 161
relaxed, 153, 154
remember, 16
remote control, 38
requesting, 136
restaurant, 47
rice, 70
ride, 19
room, 58
run, 19

S

saddened, 154
same, 102
satisfied, 154
Saturday, 12
say, 82
school, 47
a second, 85
see, 16
sell, 48
sensitive, 153
sentences
positive, 15
negative, 21
questions, 26
sharp, 39
she, 13
shirt, 37
since, 119
shocked, 154
shop, 47
should, 114
to shop, 92
short, 39
short questions, 28
shorts, 38
shut, 38
sit, 14
skirt, 38
sleep, 14
small, 38
smartphone, 38
snack, 76
sofa, 37

some, 110-111
sometimes, 145
soon, 158
sorry, 154
speak, 14
spoon, 37
strongwilled, 153
study, 92
sugar, 70
surprised, 154
Sunday, 12
suffixes, 153
superlatives, 105-107
swim, 14

T

table, 37
tablet/pad, 38
take a train, 19
tall, 39
talk, 92
tea, 70
tell, 82
telling the time, 85
that (pronoun), 43
that (modifier), 62
that (conjunction), 80
their/theirs, 43
the same as, 102
them, 13
then, 127, 128
there, 18
there are, 62
there is, 62
they, 13
these, 43
think, 14, 82
this (pronoun), 43
this (modifier), 62
those, 43
Thursday, 12
ticket, 58
time indicators, 73
time modifiers, 74
times, 57, 69, 145
today, 74
together, 133
tomorrow, 74
  day after tomorrow, 74
tones, 5
tonight, 76
too, 107, 133
train (take a), 19
travelling verbs, 19
t-shirt, 38
Tuesday, 12
TV, 38

U

umbrella, 38
unappreciated, 153
under, 116
understand, 16
until, 119
unusual, 150
upstairs, 118
us, 13
use, 92
usually, 148

V

vegetable oil, 70
verb-to-be, 43, 47, 51
verbs, 14, 16, 19, 48, 82, 92, 118, 168-172
very, 107
village, 47
vowels, 4

W

wait, 16
walk, 19
want to, 17
want to have/to get, 63
wardrobe, 37
warm, 39
water, 37
we, 13
weak, 153
Wednesday, 12
week, 73
what, 78
when, 78, 119
where, 49
which, 92
white, 40
who, 45
whose, 46
why, 79
wide, 39
will, 24
willpower, 154
window, 38
with, 22
within, 74
woman, women, 58
work, 14
would like to, 17
write, 14

Y

year, 74
  this year, 74
  next year, 74
  last year, 74
yellow, 40
yesterday, 74
  day before yesterday, 74
you, 13
your/yours, 43

Z

zero, 7

About The Authors

Ian Fereday is an Englishman who moved to Phuket, Thailand in 1991 after meeting and marrying the owner of Patong Language School. A lifelong fascination with Thai began in the first year of learning the language of his adopted country, and led to him creating and developing the study materials used in the school to teach Thai to foreigners. Now retired in Phuket, Ian still produces and constantly improves the Thai and English materials used to teach in PLS.

Rattanaporn (Bee) Pimsuwan is a Thai native from Angthong province and has been the manager of Patong Language School since 1997. Being a very busy school with hundreds of foreigners coming to learn Thai every year, Bee now has many years' experience and an in-depth understanding of how learners acquire the Thai language. Working with Ian, she helps develop and edit all the study materials used at Patong Language School.

Other books in the Thai Today series

Now that you can speak Thai, how about learning to read?

Our **Read & Write Thai Today** book is perfect for beginner learners, using a simple system we developed over 40 years that will have you reading your first words on day one.

To improve your conversation skills even further, take a look at our **Thai Tenses & Talking About Time**. An in-depth look at how to put your sentences in the correct tense for any situation.

Our books are available on Amazon and from other good booksellers.

Printed in Poland
by Amazon Fulfillment
Poland Sp. z o.o., Wrocław

54994801R00120